Badre-Eddine Ezziti

The Change Legal Status of Jews in Morocco (1856-1956)

Badre-Eddine Ezziti

The Change Legal Status of Jews in Morocco (1856-1956)

From Dhimmis to Citizens

Noor Publishing

Imprint
Any brand names and product names mentioned in this book are subject to trademark, brand or patent protection and are trademarks or registered trademarks of their respective holders. The use of brand names, product names, common names, trade names, product descriptions etc. even without a particular marking in this work is in no way to be construed to mean that such names may be regarded as unrestricted in respect of trademark and brand protection legislation and could thus be used by anyone.

Cover image: www.ingimage.com

Publisher:
Noor Publishing
is a trademark of
International Book Market Service Ltd., member of OmniScriptum Publishing Group
17 Meldrum Street, Beau Bassin 71504, Mauritius

Printed at: see last page
ISBN: 978-613-9-42915-8

Zugl. / Approved by: Ifrane, University of Akhawyn, 2016

The Changing Legal Status of Jews in Morocco (1856-1956)

Moroccan Jews Change of Status from Dhimmis to Citizens

By

Badre-Eddine EZZITI

Preface

I would like to take this opportunity to express praise and to thank Allah for giving me the opportunity to write and finish an important work of this nature. I would also like to express my heartfelt thanks to many people for their help in this particular work. First, I must express my thanks to my beloved wife who is always a source of assistance and help. I would like acknowledge the support of my family members. Special thanks to my parents, my brothers and sisters for providing me with unfailing support and continuous encouragement throughout my life. I must express my thanks to Dr. John Shoup, for his guidance helped me in all the time of writing of this work. Finally, I must say this accomplishment would not have been possible without you. Thank you.

Badre-Eddine Ezziti
Morocco, Fez
February 17, 2019

The Scope of the Study

At the beginning of the second half of the twentieth century, the legal status of non-Muslims in Morocco has changed. Moroccan Jews in particular has moved from being a "secondary nationals" in Moroccan society to citizens. In the aftermath of independence, the Moroccan regime started to acknowledge Jews as part of its essential "subjects", citizens. Through looking at historical and discursive data, this book examines the historical evolution of the legal status of Jews in Morocco with reference to the relationship between religious texts and its particular manifestations in practice. The aim is to highlight the legal status, which had been obtained by the Jews in the aftermath of independence in 1956, and how and why these changes happened. It explores the shifting relationship between the *Makhzan* and Jews in Morocco in legal terms as well as in the emergence of new discourses of "equality"which the *Makhzan* began to use to describe treatment of Jews (how Jews should be treated) between 1856 and 1956. It focuses on two periods of the modern Morocco: 1) pre-colonial period starting from 1856, when Morocco singed a treaty with the Great Britain: 2) colonial period starting from 1912 until 1956, when Morocco gained independence from France. Focusing on pre-colonial and colonial periods gives a clear picture to understanding the legal status of Jews: how it was, how it had become and how it was used during these periods. Through details examination of historical facts and events that happened during these periods, this book locates how the *Makhzen* adopted a new radical shifting in the legal status of Jews. Therefore, this book is an attempt to find an answer for questions such as how Jews moved from Dhimmis to citizens, and to what extent Jews achieve emancipation – the end to Dhimmi status.

This book provides a contribution to the legal history of religious minorities (Dhimmis) in the modern Moroccan society, and more specific to the legal aspects of Jews under Moroccan Islam. Recently, there is a considerable attention to the history of Moroccan Jews by the Moroccan State. Therefore, it attempts, on one hand, to elaborate the history of Moroccan Jews, and on the other, to explore the historical tolerance of the Moroccan sultans towards *Ahl al-Kitāb* under Islamic (Maliki) law. In addition, this book comes to fill a gap that has existed in the field of legal writings about the Moroccan Jewish communities during the French Protectorate, especially by Muslim researchers.[1] Although some research has been conducted about this topic, it is still not enough.[2] Even with these few works, they do not give attention to the legal status of Jews during this period insofar as they give to other aspects such as economy. In other words, this topic is to highlight the part of Moroccan history ignored by most Muslim historians.

---

[1] Mustapha Hassani, Mohammed Kenbib, Ahmed Twafiq, and Aomar Boum. These are some the Muslim researchers who wrote about the Jewish question in Morocco within pre and post-1956 Morocco.

[2] Mohammad Hatami, 'Moroccan Jewish Groups in scholarly research', *Religion et Société en Afrique* : le débat. (Rabat : Institut des études africaines, 2009) : 9-23.

Introduction

The Jewish legal status in Morocco has seen considerable debates among the various researchers and historians, who are interested in Moroccan Jewish history. The historical sources reflect an almost contradictory picture about the status of Jews in Morocco. Most of them, especially the European travelers who visited Morocco in the nineteenth century and the turn of the twentieth century, addressed the legal status of Moroccan Jews from a pessimistic perspective, where they look at the *dhimma* law and the misery of *mellah*.[3] In fact, they limit their studies, to comparing the status of Moroccan Jews with the status of Western Jews. They seldom link between the status of *dhimmis* in Morocco and the general socio-political framework of Morocco before colonization. In contrast to this view, other scholars hold that the legal status of Jews in Morocco was better compared with the status of Jews in Europe in the middle Ages.[4] However, both of these views agree that the nineteenth century, especially the second half, is considered as a prominent turning point in the history of Moroccan Jews. The nineteenth century was the beginning of radical changes in the improvement of the legal status of Jews in Morocco due to foreign factors and influences that had huge impacts on the general status of Jews in Morocco. At this time, the Moroccan Jewish communities had seen many changes; however, the most notable was the Jewish legal status. The focus of

[3] See Andre Chouraqui, *La Condition Juridique de L'Israelite Marocain* (Paris : 1950) and also the book of Antoine Fattal *Le statut légal des non-musulmans en pays d'Islam* (Dar al-Machreq Sarl : 1995).

[4] Simon Levy, "The Jewish Community in the Framework of the History of Morocco: from the 17th Century to the last 20th Century", *Identity and dialogue, Modern and Contemporary History of the Jews of Morocco* (Rabat: Dar Al Stoki: 1982).

this book is to highlight these changes in the light of foreign factors and influences that led to these changes in this period and those that followed.

Looking back at Jewish history in Morocco, over the centuries, and, until the establishment of French protectorate in 1912, Jews were the only religious minority who inhabited Morocco.[5] The presence of Jews in Morocco is very old, where they have lived for almost two thousand years,[6] where they settled in Morocco before the arrival of Islam.[7] They lived in nearly the all parts of Morocco where they interacted with local society - Berbers and Arabs. Morocco had the largest Jewish population in the Maghreb, where they outnumbered the Jews of Algeria and Tunisia together, although their number was no more than three percent of the total population of Morocco.[8]

Legally, politically, and socially, since the arrival of Islam in the 7th century, and following the establishment of the Idrisid dynasty at the end of the 8th country, a new Islamic culture emerged. Islam became the dominant religion in Morocco. The eighth century was the beginning of many radical changes. The arrival of Islam had significant effects on legal, political, and social aspects, especially on restructuring (reconfiguring) society. It consisted of two religious communities; the Muslim community, which represents the dominant majority, is politically active on all levels, especially on the level of the central authority represented by the

[5] Mohammed Kenbib, *Juifs et Musulmans au Maroc, 1859-1948: contribution à l'histoire des relations inter-communautaires en terre d'Islam* (Casablanca: Imprimerie Najah ElJadida, 1994), 17.

[6] Haim Zafrani, *Two Thousands Years of Jewish Life in Morocco* (Jersey City, NJ: KTAV, 2005),1.

[7] Ibid.

[8] Ibid.

dominance of the sultans; and the Jewish community, which represents the minority subjects directly to the central authority (Muslim rulers / the Sultans) in accordance with Islamic law (Dhimma Law).[9] Therefore, up to the last decade of the nineteenth century, and as is the case of all Jews of other Muslim countries, the legal status of Jews in Morocco was still determined by the Islamic teachings. They lived under the *Dhimma* law, as was drawn by classical Muslim jurists, which laid down in a contract, commonly called *al-Shurūt al-'Umariyya*[10] for nearly twelve centuries. Based on this contract, Jews were committed to certain restrictions and rules. "Some of the restrictions included: removing one's shoes in front of a mosque; being forbidden to ride a horse or other noble animal; not being allowed to bear arms; having to wear a designated costume that identified them as Jews; and always showing deference to Muslims".[11]In compliance with these restrictions, they enjoyed practicing their permitted rights such as freedom of religious worship and freedom of movement[12] and "maintained religiously autonomous institutions [such as organizing collective life and managing the synagogues][13] as long as they abided by the restrictions placed on them."[14] In return for services, which were offered them by the Moroccan state, such as protection and exemption from service in the army, they were obligated to pay a certain amount of money that agreed on by the so-called *jiziyah*.[15] In this sense, Muhammad Tahtah points

[9] Simon Levy, "The Jewish Community in the framework of the History of Morocco", 28.
[10] Sharon Vance, "The Martyrdom of a Moroccan Jewish Saint", 41.
[11] Ibid., 47.
[12] Armand Lévy, *Il Etait une Fois les Juifs Marocains*, 36
[13] Ibid.,
[14] Sharon Vance, "The Martyrdom of a Moroccan Jewish Saint", 41.
[15] 'Aṭā 'Alī Muḥammad Shiḥātah Rayyah, *al-Yahūd fī bilād al-Maghrib al-Aqṣa' fī 'Ahd al-Marīnīyīn Wa-al-Waṭṭāsīyīn* (Dimashq : Dār al-Kalimah, 1999), 23.

out that despite the fact that Jews, in return for the payment of *jiziyah*, enjoyed the protection of the government and religious freedom, they did not enjoy the effective equality with Muslim in which they had to show a respect to Muslims.[16] Antoine Fattal emphasized, in his study on the legal status of non-Muslims in Muslim lands, that

> The *dhimmi* has place in society, but he is constantly reminded of the inferiority...In no way is the *dhimmi* the equal of the Muslim. He is marked out of social inequality and belongs to a despised caste; unequal in regard to individual rights; unequal as regard taxes; unequal in the Law Courts as his evidence is not admitted by any Muslim tribunal.[17]

Additionally, they had a right to renew and rebuild their synagogues but not to establish new ones in the cities that were conquered by Muslims.[18] With regard to their internal affairs, they were "allowed to follow their own laws in governing their affairs."[19] They also had a freedom to adjudicate cases involving disputes between them in Jewish Courts based on their laws and books.[20] However, "cases involving disputes between Jews and Muslims would be adjudicated in Islamic courts where Jews were not allowed to give testimony."[21] Based on the *Dhimma* law, Jews could not, as religious minority, be assigned to political positions or be employed at work in state

[16] Muhammad Tahtah, "Brothers Enemies: the Jews of Morocco in the Modern era". 16 /01/2012. http://www.hespress.com/orbites/45471.html (Accessed 12/10/2015).

[17] Antoine Fattal, le statut legal des Musulmans en Pays d'Islam, Impromerie catholique(Beirut: 1958), 369-372 in David Littman, Bat Ye'OR, *Protected people Under Islam*, 1976, 3.

[18] 'Aṭā 'Alī Muḥammad Shiḥātah Rayyah, *al-Yahūd fī bilād al-Maghrib al-Aqṣá*, 23.

[19] Sharon Vance, "The Martyrdom of a Moroccan Jewish Saint", 42.

[20] 'Aṭā 'Alī Muḥammad Shiḥātah Rayyah, *al-Yahūd fī bilād al-Maghrib al-Aqṣá*, 24.

[21] Sharon Vance, "The Martyrdom of a Moroccan Jewish Saint", 42.

offices. They mainly worked at crafts that were considered socially low status such as carpentry and gold craft. However, as Armand Levy, in his book on Moroccan Jews stressed, "the *dhimma* restrictions have not been always followed literarily in Morocco."[22] Moroccan history has shown many of the cases in which "rules in many Moroccan dynasties appointed Jews to positions of authority in their courts."[23] Through the historical and jurisprudential writings clearly illustrated that Jews occupied important positions in the Moroccan state, especially during the Marinide (1421-1465), Wattasid (1472-1554), and Alaouite (from 1635 until now) dynasties. During the time of Abd al-Haqq II, "who was a sultan of Morocco from 1421 until 1465,"[24] there were many Jews who were appointed to high positions in the state. The sultan of the Marinide,[25] Abd al-Haqq b. Abu Sa'id "had a Jewish Vizier, Harun ben Batas,"[26] who was a responsible for the economic affairs.[27] He also appointed a Jew as a minister, and there was another Jew who occupied the position of the chief of police.[28] Concerning the Wattasid sultans, they also appointed many Jews as ministers and used others on a political mission abroad. For example, Ya'qub Rosales was appointed as an ambassador of the Sultan Ahmed b. Muhammad II to the King of Portugal in 1530 and 1538. The same Sultan sent a Jew for a political mission to Spain in 1530.[29] Concerning the Alawite dynasty, sources are full of stories that indicate the high standing of Jews in the state. Take as an

---

[22] Armand Lévy, *Il Etait une Fois les Juifs Marocains*, 36.
[23] Sharon Vance, "The Martyrdom of a Moroccan Jewish Saint", 47.
[24] David Corcos, "the Jews of Morocco under the Marinides", *The Jewish Quarterly Review, New Series*, Vol. 54, No. 4 (April, 1964), 271.
[25] Marinides, as European historians term them.
[26] Ibid.
[27] 'Aṭā 'Alī Muḥammad Shiḥātah Rayyah, *al-Yahūd fī bilād al-Maghrib al-Aqṣá*, 50.
[28] Ibid.,52.
[29] Ibid., 57.

example the time of Sultan Moulay Ismail (1672-1727); He appointed a senior Jewish figure named Abraham Maimoran as a minister.[30] The Sultan Moulay Suliman (1792-18822) appointed two Jews ministers in his government. He also appointed other Jews as ambassadors to represent Morocco abroad;[31] however, "and in doing so often provoked the reprobation of the *'ulama* who considered such appointments to be violations of Islamic law."[32]

Furthermore, the sources, especially the books of *Fatawa* that are known in Morocco as *al-Nawazil al-Fiqhiyah*, indicate many cases, where Jews did not remain linked to the religious requirements literally as the case of Jews in several Saharan Oases, but sometimes they escape from the *Dhimma* restrictions with the help of Sultans. In Saharan Oases, Jews "dressed like Muslims and made trading journeys with the company of Muslims, riding horses,"[33] had their own synagogues, and built news synagogues. They also did not pay *jiziyah* to state.[34] John Hunwick, in his work on *Jews of a Saharan Oasis: Eliminations of the Tamantit Community*, quotes several *Fatawa* of Maliki jurists who condemned this situation such as the *mufti* Ibn Zakari (d.1495), the *Qadi* Muhammad al-'Uqbani (d.1467), and Abd al-Karim al-Maghili.[35] Hunwick states that "in the 1480s, Muhammad B. 'Abd al-Jabbar al-Figigi, a scholar from oasis of Figuig, addressed a question to Qadi al-'Asnuni concerning the legal status of the

---

[30] Muhammad Tahtah, "Brothers Enemies", 16 /01/2012. http://www.hespress.com/orbites/45471.html (Accessed 12/10/2015).

[31] Ibid.

[32] Sharon Vance, "the Martyrdom of a Moroccan Jewish Saint", 47.

[33] John Hunwick, *Jews of a Saharan Oasis: Eliminations of the Tamantit Community* (Princeton: Markus Wiener Publishers, 2006), 11.

[34] 'Aṭā 'Alī Muḥammad Shiḥātah Rayyah, *al-Yahūd fī bilād al-Maghrib al-Aqṣá*, 44.

[35] John Hunwick, *Jews of a Saharan Oasis*, 11.

synagogues existing in several Saharan *qusur*.[36] 'Alī Muḥammad Shiḥātah, in his work on *al-Yahūd fī bilād al-Maghrib al-Aqṣá*, points out that the Marinide sultan, Abu al-Hassan, abolished *jiziyah*, and he did not ask Jews to pay *jiziyah* due to their good behavior towards the state.[37]

On the other hand, this is does not mean that Jews often received good treatment and were protected from harm based on the *Dhimma* law. But there were several periods in which Jews suffered and faced difficult times, sometimes by some rulers and sometimes by the *'ulama* and Muslim population. In the twelfth century, "the Almohad Dynasty was a period of forced conversion and religious persecution that exceeded the restrictions delineated in the Pact and even violated the Qur'anic injunctions against religious persecution."[38] Rick Gold shows this fact by stating that "They did not take the Jews under their protection. Instead, they expelled them from Marrakesh and tried to eliminate their presence from Morocco."[39] They "showed no mercy to any coreligionist of their disinclined to follow their lead and destroyed every vestige of Jewish life."[40] For instance, "the Jewish communities in the oases communities of Sijilmassa and Dara, under the Almohad Caliph Abd al-Moumen (1130–1163) were destroyed and Jews who did not convert to Islam were killed." According to Rick Gold, "by 1224, there may have been no synagogue left in the Almohads."[41] This experience repeated in the last decade of 18th century under the Alawite sultan Mawaly

[36] Ibid,.33

[37] 'Aṭā 'Alī Muḥammad Shiḥātah Rayyah, *al-Yahūd fī bilād al-Maghrib al-Aqṣá*, 44.

[38] Sharon Vance, The Martyrdom of a Moroccan Jewish Saint, 47.

[39] Rick Gold, Arab and Berber Dynasties from the 7th to the 17th Century, http://rickgold.home.mindspring.com/page8.html (Accessed 12/12/2015).

[40] David Corcos, the Jews of Morocco under the Marinides, 284.

[41] Rick Gold, Arab and Berber Dynasties from the 7th to the 17th Century, http://rickgold.home.mindspring.com/page8.html (Accessed 12/12/2015).

al-Yazid (1790-1792), who "allowed many Jewish quarters to be plundered, especially the *Mellah* of Tetouan, as well as persecution of many of those who served his father,[42] Sidi Muhammad. These narratives have shown that the history of Jews in Morocco had a varied record of the enforcement of the *dhimma* requirements and show in many examples Moroccan rulers and religious scholars reinterpreted certain components of restrictions such as wearing a distinct dress or destroying the Jews' houses worship. Hence, one should remember the statements of Armand Levy on the legal status of Jews in Morocco. The spirit of tolerance that is the doctrine of Islamic law, in Morocco, depends on the good or ill will of the sultans and the representatives of the *Makhzen*. However, the jurisprudential procedures could at any moment fall upon the *dhimmis*.[43] Generally, the tolerance of the Jews was greater in practice than in theory. In Morocco, according to this legal position (Dhimma), the Jewish communities were subject to two authorities: the sultans (central authority) and regional authority in the large cities. In addition to the tribute to the royal treasury, they had to pay the Sultan the same as Muslim subjects such as gifts on occasions.[44]

In contrast to the previous centuries, starting from the nineteenth century, particularly in the second half, the Jewish community saw several radical shifts. In this period, many external influences and factors began to destabilize the traditional Islamic system in Morocco. However, the most major destabilizing force is the emergence of the status of consular protection offered by foreign powers to many Jewish merchants. This new status "was a direct challenge to Muslim authority and sovereignty, [where]

[42] Mohamed El Mansour, *Morocco in the reign of Mawaly Sulayman*, 14.
[43] Armand Lévy. *Il Etait une Fois les Juifs Marocains*, 36.
[44] Ibid., 31.

the protection offered by the foreign powers began to challenge that offered by the Islamic state as represented by the sultan."[45] In this respect, the visit of Sir Moses Montefiore, a leader of Britain's Jewish Community, was considered as the turning point for the beginning of improving the legal status of the Moroccan Jewish community. His visit to Sultan Muhammad b. 'Abd al-Rahman, in Marrakesh in 1864 was to pressure the sultan into improving the legal status of Jews by stressing reforms that "would eliminate the legal disabilities associated with Dhimmi status."[46] In the aftermath of this meeting, the sultan issued the first *dahir* concerning the issue of the Jewish relationship to the state on February 5, 1864. Although this *zahir* did not add anything new to what Islam had decided before about *Ahl al-Kitāb*, the sultan, by doing this, acquired British friendship.[47] The full text of this *zahir* is in the book entitled *Kitāb al-Istiqsa* by the Moroccan historian from that period Ahmed al-Nasiri.[48] On the other hand, the consular protection (the foreign protection), in turn, is considered as another turning point in the legal changes of the status of Jews in Morocco. Thus, it was the major problem that the *Makhzan* (Moroccan government) faced in the second half of the nineteenth century. It was another way to escape the restrictions of Islamic law. After the Jews obtained foreign protection, they enjoyed several legal privileges such as the nationality of the country that provided this protection. This new position of those Jews forced the *Makhzan* to rethink in the treatment of Jews who were still

[45] Daniel J. Schroeter, "From Dhimmis to Colonized Subjects: Moroccan Jews and the Sharifian and French Colonial State," *Studies in Contemporary Jewry*, 19 (2003), 111.

[46] Ibid.

[47] Norman A. Stillman, *the Jews of Arab Lands in Modern Times* (New York: the Jewish Publication Society, 1991), 14.

[48] Ahmed al-Nasiri, *Kitāb al-Istiqsa fi Maghreb al-qsa* (Casablanca: Dar al-Kitāb, 1956), 112-114, translated in Stillman, *Jews of Arab lands*, pp. 371-73.

subject to the sultan. In addition, the Madrid Treaty resulting from the Conference of 1888 is also considered as a turning point of civil status changes of Jews where it included an article 15 that recognized the concept of nationality for Moroccans: both Jews and Muslims.[49] In this framework and seeking to enjoy a new status and be free from the traditional Islamic legal framework, the beginning of the twentieth century was another turning point in the history of Moroccan Jews. Believing that the best way of emancipation from Islamic restrictions is the European protection, Moroccan Jews, especially the elites, "welcomed the protectorate, hoping that the French would not only provide greater security but would also extend civil rights to the Jewish community."[50] However, the French authorities in Morocco, under the Resident General Hubert Lyautey, declined to change the status of the Jews and preferred to retain them in the framework of their previous status inside Moroccan society. [51] This decision ignited a great dissatisfaction among the Jewish communities because it created a kind of confusion and nebulous position in the legal status of Moroccan Jews.[52] Theoretically, the notion of the establishment of protectorate means reforming the legal status not replacing them for colonized subjects. In fact, by this decision, Jews were excluded from the picture, where they lost their former status and at the same time their autonomy in which they became not even referred of as Moroccans or as French.[53] Therefore, instead of asking the French authorities to eliminate

[49] Daniel J. Schroeter and Joseph Chetrit, "Emancipation and its Discontents: Jews at the formative Period of Colonial Rule in Morocco," *Jewish Social Studies: History, Culture, Society* n. s. 13, no. 1 (2006): 177.

[50] Daniel J. Schroeter, "From Dhimmis to Colonized Subjects," 111.

[51] Muhammad Kenbib, *Juifs et Musulmans au Maroc*, 29.

[52] Daniel J. Schroeter and Joseph Chetrit, "Emancipation and its Discontents," 206.

[53] Muhammad Kenbib, *Juifs et Musulmans au Maroc*, 113.

the Dhimmi status and implement reforms, they turned to the sultan to ask for him to protect them under the Dhimmi law at the time of application of the Vichy anti-Jewish legislation on Moroccan Jews in 1942.

The problematic mentioned above frames the focus of this book. This book intends to explore the legal status that frames the Moroccan Jews' relationship to the sultan/ *Makhzan* in the second half of the nineteenth century and also to the French authorities in the first half of the twentieth century. It is also an attempt to examine the dynamic through which the legal status of Jews changed from Dhimmis to citizens.

The central research question addressed is the legal status that regulates the relationship between the Jewish community and the Moroccan state accorded to Dhimmi (Jews) in the modern Moroccan society (1856-1956). There are several sub questions here. (1) How does the Dhimmi law regulate the relationship between the Muslims and the People of the Book in an Islamic state? (2)What is the legal relationship between Jews and Moroccan state within the pre and during colonial period? (3) How was the status of Dhimmi used by the three parties; the French authorities, the Moroccan State, and the Jews? (4) How did legal changes at the center affect the status of Jews in rural or periphery regions differently? (5) To what extent does the French intervention in the Moroccan administration form a real improvement in the situation for Jews? The ultimate aim of this research is to contribute to the legal history of Jews in Morocco, which was often described as degrading treatment, and to grasp a better understanding of the reasons of the evolution of the legal status. On the other hand, it is to reveal the existing contradiction in the interpretation of Dhimmi law. In practice, the aim is to show the likely gap between the level of texts and its applied formulas in reality.

There are many reasons for limiting the framework of this book in these periods (1856-1956) to conduct research. The 19th century had seen the beginning of discussion on the legal status of Moroccan Jews, but after the establishment of the protectorate in Morocco 1912 began deliberations on the subject of Jewish communities intensified. Therefore, these years had seen the real start of many factors and events that were directly affected the status of to Jews in Morocco. The 19th century, especially the second half, and the first half of the 20th century, in Morocco considered the difficult periods in which Moroccan Jews suffered and witnessed many pressures and the arbitrary practices. If the 19th century brought emancipation to the Jews of many countries, in Morocco it failed to fundamentally change the legal status of Moroccan Jews. But, the 19th century brought new divisions among them that led to the emergence of new sources of trouble. In addition to that European powers, especially France, in those periods, began to intervene in many countries of North Africa to achieve the idea of imperialism. This European penetration brought to Moroccan Jews many of troubles and also led to instability in Moroccan society.

Additionally, instability and divisions in Morocco also contributed to fueling conflicts, for which Jews were frequent scapegoats. During the 19th century, Moroccan Jews suffered every war that Morocco involved in with foreign countries. For instance, "the war with France in 1844 brought new misery and ill treatment upon the Moroccan Jews. When the war with Spain broke out on September 22, 1859, the Muslims had nothing more fitting to do than to plunder the houses of friendly Jewish families in Tetuan". Most of the Jews saved their lives only by fleeing. About 400 were killed. A like result followed the conflict with Spain in 1853 in consequence of the violent acts of the cliff-dwellers in Melilla.

Furthermore, these periods had seen the emergence of many International organizations of Jews that were interested in Moroccan Jews. So, choosing exactly these years is because that these years are very informative and provides useful information which help in doing research. In addition, the aim of limiting of this thesis in these years is to conduct a comparison between the period of precolonial and the period of colonial to know to what extent the French intervention in the Moroccan administration forms a real improvement in the situation for Jews. Generally, selection of these years is only a matter of technique in order to determine the general framework of the research.

Literature Review

This literature review explores academic works addressing the relationship between Muslims and non-Muslims (*Ahl al-Dhimma*), in the Islamic state (*Dar al-Islam*). This is in order to find relevant arguments from different theoretical approaches, adopted by scholars on this topic. This review will focus on earlier literature as well as modern literature, which can be relevant to the main argument of this book. What was the legal status of Jews in precolonial and colonial Morocco? In addition to historical literature with interest in the Jewish issue in Morocco, this book will also make use of numerous treatises on Maliki jurisprudence. The order of the literature is based on how they are used in this book. Therefore, this literature review examines academic literature concerning two topics: 1) the nature of writings pertaining to Moroccan Jews; 2) the nature of Dhimmis, citizenship and *jiziyah.*

The Nature of Writings pertaining to Moroccan Jews.

Until recently, very little research has been conducted on the issues relating to the legal changes of Moroccan Jews in colonial and postcolonial era. Most academic works on the Jewish history revolved around two traditions of academic research.[54] One is, following the first years of independence, Moroccan postcolonial scholarly research focuses on the Moroccan history and ethnography in which the history of Jews has been ignored for over three decades.

Addressing the issue of writings pertaining to Jews, in an article written in 2009, Muhammad Hatimi argues that Jewish people have often been ignored in scholarly research where there was no research or dissertation concerning an aspect of Jewish history had been done. He writes that "during the first years of Moroccan independence, studies focused on highlighting the historical roots of the Moroccan nation and rooting of the elements of the legitimacy of the Moroccan state".[55] Thus, Moroccan postcolonial scholarly research did not deal with specific themes of Jews in Morocco. They mostly discuss the news of Jews in the midst of the

[54] Alan R. Meyers, "Patronage and protection: the status of Jews in precolonial Morocco", in S. Deshen and W.P. Zenner (eds), *Jewish Societies in the Middle East* (Washington DC: University Press of America, 1982), 83.

[55] Mohammad Hatami, 'Moroccan Jewish Groups in scholarly research', *Religion et Société en Afrique : le débat.* (Rabat : Institut des études africaines, 2009), 17.

major events is listed, with some details in the events which have seen the involvement of Jews.[56] The second tradition of scholarly research has studied the Moroccan Jewish history and their social life "with some reference to the boarder historical, social, cultural, and political context within which this history has taken place".[57] Indeed, these two traditions do not recognize the participations of Jews in society and do not show their integration in their surrounding society. But, they show that Jewish people were always secondary participants.

Another scholar who addressed the issue is Allan R. Meyers. In his article written in 1982, *Patronage and Protection: the Status of Jews in Precolonial Morocco*, Meyers comments on these two traditions of academic works by arguing that "each of these scholarly traditions has produced studies of lasting and even monumental importance, but neither has been able to adequately set Moroccan Jewish communities in their Moroccan milleux".[58] However, recently, there are several modern sociologists, anthropologists and historians from different nationalities who try to break down this method of those works. They try to rebuild Moroccan Jewish history, mainly to determine the impacts that affected the legal status in late nineteenth and early twentieth countries (Allan R. Meyres, 1982; Daniel J. Schroeter, 2003; 2006; Yigal Bin-Nun, 2010; Jessica Marglin, 2010; Aomar Boum, 2011; 2012; 2013). On the other hand, some scholars and historians go far beyond that in which they have begun to study the identity of Moroccan Jews in the context of Moroccan Islam (Daniel J. Schroeter, 2007; 2008; Yaron Tsur, 2011, Emily Benichou Gottreich, 2013; Jessica Marglin,

[56] Ibid.
[57] Alan R. Meyers, 'Patronage and protection, 83.
[58] Ibid.

2011; 2012). As these dates of these academic works indicate, in recent decade, there is a significant academic literature that provides a great deal of data about the issue pertaining to the legal status of Jews and the influences of the events that happened in precolonial or colonial Morocco on the legal changes. Some of these academic works are reviewed in this section. In this regard, it is important to mention to a great work on the legal pluralism and Jews in Morocco during nineteenth century that conducted recently by Jessica Marglin. Her work is a dissertation that was presented to the faculty Princeton University in candidacy for the degree of Doctor of Philosophy in January 2013, entitled *In the Courts of the Nations: Jews, Muslims, and Legal Pluralism in the Nineteenth-century Morocco*. As she writes in her abstract, this work considered as "the first study of Jews' legal strategies in precolonial Morocco based on archival evidence [because] it examines the participation of Jews in Morocco's legal system during the long nineteenth century up to 1912". However, this work has not been published yet.

The Nature of the Concepts of Dhimmis, Citizenship and Jiziyah Pertaining to Modernity

This is an overview of the academic literature focusing on the nature of concepts of Dhimmi, citizenship (nationality), and *jiziyah* pertaining to modernity. It is well known between researchers that the origin of Dhimma is the Quran, the verse 9:29, which is *"fight against those who (1) believe not in Allah, (2) nor in the last Day, (3) nor forbid that which has been forbidden by Allah and His messenger (4) and those who acknowledge not the religion of truth among the people of the scripture, until they pay the jiziyah with willing submission, and feel themselves subdued".* This verse is recognized as the origin of the Dhimma law even if does not mention directly to the word of Dhimma. Thus, the Dhimma law has the principals that regulate the relationship between Muslims and non-Muslims. So, under this status non-Muslims enjoyed many rights such as "freedom to practice their religious rituals, freedom of religion and the right to renovate [and to erect their] houses of worship."[59] Recently, an extensive debate has emerged about the concept of Dhimma among the Muslim scholars whether to abolish it altogether, amend it, or maintain it." [60] One of the contemporary Muslim thinker addressed this issue is Rachid al-Ghannoushi, in his book entitled *Public Freedoms in the Islamic State*, published in 1998, discusses this issue and reaches a conclusion that the concept of Dhimma is not included among the words that are mandatory in Shari'a.[61] Thus, he argues that this concept can be replaced by any other concept in order to avoid the confusion such as the concept of citizenship as long as achieves the principle of equality among citizens.[62] In the same line, Muhammad Salim al-'Awa , in his article written in 2003 entitled *Dhimmis in the Islamic Legal System, Contemporary Islamic Vision* and his book entitled *Religion and the Homeland: Chapters in the Relation between Muslims and non-Muslim,* published in 2009, reviews the problems brought by modernity about the Dhimma law. In both works, he argues that it is time to reform the law of Dhimma to keep up with

[59] Ilia Alon, "Dhimma", *Encyclopedia of the Modern Middle East and North Africa*. 2004. Encyclopedia.com. http://www.encyclopedia.com/doc/1G2-3424600816.html (accessed November 25, 2013).

[60] Ibid.

[61]. Rached Ghannouchi., *Public freedoms in the Islamic state* (Beirut: Central studies for Arab Unity, 1998), 290-291.

[62] Ibid.

modernity, especially with the emergence of the concept of citizenship.[63] In the same direction, an article written in 1994 by Sudanese Tariq al-Bashir entitled *Dhimmis in the Islamic Legal System, Contemporary Islamic Vision* argues.[64] This debate between Muslim scholars about the Dhimma and the possibility of the reforms of the Dhimma law accordance with modernity by adapting the concept of citizenship with the Islamic jurisprudence also took place in the west.

Among the western scholars who discuss this issue is Andrew F. March in his book entitled *Islam and Liberal Citizenship: the Search for an Overlapping Consensus, published in 2009.* In the Western contexts, "citizenship is a legal status that bestows uniform rights and duties upon all members of a state."[65] Based on this definition, March argues that "the Islamic jurisprudence is opposite to liberal citizenship in three parts: the problem of residing, the problem of loyalty to such a state and the problem of solidarity."[66] From this argument, we argue that the concept of Dhimmi in the Islamic jurisprudence is opposite to the definition of the liberal citizenship that was mentioned above, especially in terms of religious affiliation.

[63] "Dhimmis in the Islamic legal system, contemporary Islamic vision", *Journal of the good life* 32, no. 11 (2003). And also his book on: *religion and the homeland: chapters in the relation between Muslims and non-Muslims* (Cairo: Dar Nahdet, 2009).

[64] "About the conditions of participation in the public affairs of State to non-Muslims in contemporary Islamic societies", *Journal of Modern Muslim* 69 and 72, no. 5 (January 2, 1994).

[65]. Gall Bossenga,"Citizenship." Europe, 1450 to 1789: Encyclopedia of the Early Modern World. 2004. Encyclopedia.com. http://www.encyclopedia.com/doc/1G2-3404900219.html (accessed December 6, 2013).

[66]. Andrew F. March, *Islam and Liberal Citizenship: the Search for an Overlapping Consensus* (Oxford University Press, 2009), 106.

In one of the most important classical academic work on Islamic law entitled *Ahkam al-Dhimma wa al-Musta'manin fi Dar al-Islam*, published 1982, Abd al- Karim Zaydan details the rights and duties of non-Muslims (*Ahl al-Dhimma and Musta'min*–protected one) in an Islamic state.[67] Among the themes that the author discusses is the issue of nationality of Dhimmi in Islam. He dedicates two chapters discussing the nationality of *Ahl al-Dhimma*. In the context of the enjoyment of the nationality of *Dar al-Islam* or not for *Ahl al-Dhimma*, Zaydan argues that *ahl al-Dhimma* enjoy the nationality and citizenship of Dar al-Islam as Muslims and both of them have the same rights and duties except for what is related to the beliefs and rituals. So, according to the author, Dhimmis have the right to engaged and participate in all actions/fields such as politics and economy of the state except for what is related to religion.[68]The main feature of his study is that it addresses two kinds of non-Muslims, *Ahl al-Dhimma* who are required to pay *jiziyah* and non-Muslims (*Musta'min*), who come to an Islamic state for some reasons as visitors or students wanting to learn.

With regard to *jiziyah* (Arab., *jazā*, 'reward, requite'), it also based on the Qur'an 9:29, which is *"fight against those who (1)believe not in Allah, (2) nor in the last Day, (3) nor forbid that which has been forbidden by Allah and His messenger (4) and those who acknowledge not the religion of truth among the people of the scripture, until the pay the jiziyah with willing submission, and feel themselves subdued".* Recently, *jiziyah* has also become a debatable

[67] It is a theoretical state. The author is talking generally without referring to any specific state at a specific time.

[68] Abd al- Karim Zaydan, *al-Dmmiin wa-al Musta'min fi Dar al-Islam* (Beirut: maktbat 9uds, 1982), 65.

issue between contemporary Muslim scholars whether to abolish it or to amend it.

The contemporary scholar Yusuf al-Qaradawi, in his book entitled *Non-Muslims in Muslim Society,* published in 1977, argues that

> *Jiziyah* is in return of the military service. However, if this military service has become a part of the duties of all citizens regardless their religion, Islamic states have to abolish *jiziyah* because there is no reason to keep it. In addition, our modern Islamic countries [69] based on citizenship, which one of its principles is that all inhabitants, regardless their religion, share the same duties. Otherwise, they all participated in the liberation of the country from occupation as well. Thus, the issue of liberation replaced the concept of conquest that was the main concept that the Islamic state based on.[70]

In practice, this argument is not new because the Ottoman Empire applied this rule in the earlier period. "In 1855, the Ottoman Empire abolished *jiziyah* as part of reforms to equalize the status of Muslims and non-Muslims. It was replaced, however, by a military-exemption tax on non-Muslims."[71] In addition, there are some traditional books of Islamic law told the story of Jews of Medina in the time of the Prophet where the Prophet abolished *jiziyah* and did not take it from them.

---

[69] He talks here about the Islamic state theoretically because he was not talking of a specific place.

[70] Yusuf al-Qaradawi, *Non-Muslims in Muslim society* (Cairo: Library of Wahba, 1977), 36.

[71] Thompson Elizabeth. "*jizya.*" *Encyclopedia of the Modern Middle East and North Africa.* 2004. Encyclopedia.com. http://www.encyclopedia.com/doc/1G2-3424601439.html (accessed 18 Apr. 2016).

One of these works is the book *Ahkam Ahl al-Dhimma* by Muhammad ibn Abu Bakr ibn Qayyim al-Jawziyyah, (1292-1350). The author focuses on the Islamic regulations for Jews, Christians, and groups outside of *Ahl al-Kitāb* who live in an Islamic State.[72] In terms of the questions of *jiziyah* and if is it a special for the People of Book, he argues that *jiziyah* is not for Jews and Christian only, but everyone who is not Muslim living in Muslim country is required to pay *jiziyah* even if he does not have any religion.[73] This point of view is opposite to the opinion that sees *jiziyah* is a special for the People of Book. Another question about *jiziyah* that was raised by the author is why the Prophet did not take *jiziyah* from the Jews of Medina, or from the Jewish community of Khaybar.[74] To avoid several interpretations, the author makes a technical answer where he says that was "because the Prophet signed an agreement with Jews (reconciled) before the verse of *jiziyah* come down".[75] In fact, this issue is debated between scholars, especially about the hand-written document of Imam 'Ali. This document shows that the Prophet dropped *jiziyah* on the Jews of Khaybar. Form these theoretical discussions and practical applications, it is very clear that modern Muslim scholars have to work on such issues to find a way to adopt a new *fiqh* and find solutions to the modern issues that impose themselves on the reality.

Although these reviewed academic works talk generally and do not deal with specific localities or Dhimmis of Morocco, the theoretical

---

[72] The author is using this term to refer to Dar al-Islam. Thus, the author here is talking at purely theoretical level, and he is not referring to any specific state at a specific time, but he is talking in general. In addition, early Muslim scholars divide the world generally to two parts; dar-Islam and dar al-Harb. The author is one of those scholars.

[73] Muhammad ibn Abu Bakr ibn Qayyim al-Jawziyyah, *ahkam ahl al-Dhimma*, 89.

[74] The oasis of Khaybar located 150 kilometers from Medina in the north-western part of the Arabian Peninsula, in modern-day Saudi Arabia.

[75] Muhammad ibn Abu Bakr ibn Qayyim al-Jawziyyah *, ahkam ahl al-Dhimma* , 90

information they provide is applicable to this thesis. Therefore, to relate these theoretical arguments of Islamic literature to modern literature that specialize on Morocco, we turn to review some works which was conducted on the legal system of Moroccan Jews by anthropologists, sociologists, and historians.

The earliest works on the legal status in Morocco go back to the early 1950s. The book, *The Social and Legal Status of the Jews of French Morocco,* examines the status of Jews under the French Protectorate. The author, in describing the status of Jews in colonial Morocco, writes:

> Even today, after forty years of improvement under the French, the Jews do not enjoy the privileges and advantages, for example, enjoyed by 300,000 Europeans. Nor do they have the rights, the security and the feeling of belonging enjoyed by some eight million Moslems—Berbers and Arabs—who are the subjects of the Sultan.[76]

By such these statements Andre Chouraqui opens his book to describe the status of Jews and the changes that happened under the French Protectorate. Among the themes that Chouraqui discusses, the problems of Moroccan citizenship and nationality. He says that the problems of Moroccan citizenship did not concern just Jews but also Muslims; however, for Jews the problems of Moroccan citizenship "are the key to the inferior

[76] Andre Chouraqui, *the Social and Legal Status of the Jews of French Morocco* (New York: American Jewish Committee, 1953), 20.

legal status of the Jews".[77] He continues explaining by saying that the complexity of Moroccan citizenship increased "by the application of both Western and Islamic legal principles".[78] This book is useful in showing how Jews moved from Dhimmis to that of citizens.

Another academic work that covers the factors that led to the changes in the status of Jews is the work of Simon Levy entitled *Essais d'histoire et de civilisation judeo-marocains,* published in 2001. Levy in a chapter entitled "the *Jewish Community in the Framework of the History of Morocco: from the 17th Century to the Last 20th Century"* examines the evolution of the Jewish community from the 17th century until the last quarter of the 20th century. He focuses mainly on the legal status of Jews and the relationship between them and the sultans. In his speaking about the status of Dhimma, he argues that a person cannot judge this status without looking at the historical context. Thus, we should appreciate/look at the status of Dhimmi in Morocco whether from the angle of it is as a symbol of tolerance or concerning the standards of the Universal Declaration of Human Rights.[79] He mentions to numbers of factors that led to the legal evolution during precolonial and colonial Morocco. He says that the status of consular protection is considered as the first step of evolution of the legal status[80]where protected Jews were no longer under Islamic law even if they were still having problems of citizenship.

[77] Ibid.

[78] Ibid.

[79] Simon Lévy, *Essais d'histoire et de civilisation judeo-marocains* (Rabat : Centre Tarik Ibn Zyad, 2001), 103.

[80] Ibid,. 121.

Among some articles that have been of great usefulness to this thesis is Daniel J. Schroeter's article entitled *From Dhimmis to Colonized Subjects: Moroccan Jews and the Sharifian and French Colonial State* written in 2003. Schroeter mainly analyses the nature of Moroccan Jews and the state's relationship in precolonial and colonial Morocco in which he describes the complexity of this relationship in French Protectorate for Morocco. The feature of this article is it does not focus on the French Protectorate period only, but it tries to compare between precolonial and colonial Jewish status to show to what extent Jews achieved emancipation – the end to Dhimmi status. For the author there was no emancipation for Jews in the colonial rule in Morocco. Therefore, He argues that although in precolonial times "Jews, as *ahl al-Dhimma*, were considered to be religiously inferior and contemptible,"[81] they had the autonomy of their communal institution. However, in the French Protectorate, Jews lost "some of the privileges it had enjoyed in precolonial day.'[82] Thus, for Schroeter, the reforms that French Protectorate did were not to liberate Jews from the old system, but "the primary goal of French policy toward Moroccan Jews was to control them in a very discreet manner, and thus, they lost a large measure of their former privileged autonomy."[83] From the author's discussion we can understand how the status of Jews shifts from the subjects of the sultan to become colonized subjects.

More similarity with the previous articles that has been also a great of usefulness is Joseph Chetrit and Daniel J. Schroeter' s article entitled *Emancipation and Its Discontents: Jews at the Formative Period of Colonial*

81 Daniel J. Schroeter, "From Dhimmis to Colonized Subjects", 106.
82 Ibid., 114.
83 Ibid.

Rule in Morocco, written in 2006. The focus of this article is on the period of French Protectorate in Morocco; therefore, it helps a lot in understanding the general policy of French Protectorate toward Moroccan Jews. It mostly covers all legal and social reforms that were done in the aftermath of the establishment of French protectorate until the independence. After the authors detail in the events and the reforms that took place by the French protectorate, they reach a conclusion that "the meaning of the legal [...] reforms were much more ambiguous and tentative than the term implies."[84] In terms of Moroccan citizenship for Jews, the authors comment by saying that it "had existed since its recognition at the Madrid Conference of 1888"[85] [for both Jews and Muslims]. Therefore, the question is why Moroccan Jews see the French Protectorate as vehicle to accomplish emancipation if citizenship was already recognized for them?

Haïm Zafrani's book entitled *Two Thousand Years of Jewish Life in Morocco*, published in 2005, Robert Assaraf's book entitled *Muhammad V et les juifs du Maroc à l'époque de Vichy*, published in 1997, and Muhammad Kenbib's book entitled *Juifs et Musulmans au Maroc, 1859-1948: contribution à l'histoire des relations inter-communautaires en terre d'Islam* in 1994, cover almost every aspect of Jewish life in Morocco. Zafrani mainly addresses the history of Jews by detailing throughout five chapters, the rich history of the social, economic, and intellectual life in the Jewish community. In terms of the Dhimmi status, he argues that although what was said about it (it was precarious and degrading status), "it was a liberal legal status (providing a very high degree of legal, administrative, and cultural

[84] Daniel J. Schroeter and Joseph Chetrit, "Emancipation and its Discontents", 206.
[85] Ibid.,197.

autonomy) as compared with [...] Jews under Christians in Ashkenazi lands."[86] Assaraf's book focuses mainly on the issue of the relationship between Sultan Muhammad V and Jewish communities in Morocco. Assaraf argues that there was a close relationship, which exists throughout the centuries, between the Moroccan sultans and Moroccan Jews, especially the sultans of Alawite dynasty who provide the necessary protection for Moroccan Jews. He shows, as an example, the significant attitude of Muhammad V towards Jews when he opposed to the implementation the racist policies of the Vichy government in 1941. Kenbib also covers the history of Jews in Morocco before and during the French protectorate. For the author the chronological framework is a critical period in the evolution the Jewish-Muslim relations in Morocco.

Methodology

The aim of book is to study the historical development of the legal status of Jews in pre-colonial and colonial Morocco. Since it is dedicated to the historical study and the political study of the civil and legal status of Moroccan Jews, the method which will be employed in this research is the historical analysis of the development of the legal status of Moroccan Jews. The aim of using this method, on one hand, is to help in understanding and interpretation of several historical events and documents by which will develop a narrative about this topic. On the other hand, since it will be used, in this book, the questions such as how these changes occur in the legal status of Jews, why this changed happened and how the legal status were influenced by the historical events that happened, the historical analysis

[86] Haim Zafrani, *Two Thousands Years of Jewish Life in Morocco* (Jersey City, NJ: KTAV, 2005), 4.

method is a good tool in providing answer to such questions. In addition, to come up with a good conclusion requires comprehending the scholarly arguments on a specific topic, so the historical analysis is useful in the process. Therefore, to apply this method on this topic, this book refers to numerous of historical events and facts to examine the factors that led to this development in the legal status of Moroccan Jews. It also includes the analysis of the religious opinions. For instance, Muslim scholars' arguments on the legal changes of the Dhimma law pertaining to modernity are analyzed.

The collection of data relies on primary and secondary scholarly sources. Regarding the primary sources, this book is a critical analysis of the traditional and contemporary studies on Islamic law pertaining to Dhimma status. Thus, it relies on the classical works of Islamic law but it will refer only to Maliki jurisprudence. On the other hand, this book will not look at the source of Islamic law from the religious' point of view, but as sources of the history that dates for certain periods of the legal status of *Ahl al-Dhimma*. Thus, this book does not support any opinion of a specific scholar. Second sources of data were from the secondary sources. They are composed of specialized academic literature such as historical books, journal and magazine articles on the subject of Moroccan Jews. Additionally, this book relies on online sources.

There are several variables that will be measured in this book. These variables include Dhimmis, citizenship, and *jiziyah*. They were explored throughout the study of the three chapters of book from both Muslim scholars' and Western scholars' point of view.

In order to understand how and why this change happened in the nature of the Jewish legal status, it is important to consider the general framework of the legal status of Jews in Moroccan Islam up to 1856. Another important issue that is also necessary to consider is the general status of Jews in 1856, and the nature of relations between Jews and Moroccan sultans and also between Jews and Europe in the 1856. It is also necessary to consider the general situation of Moroccan politics and its relations with the foreign powers, especially European power at that time. In addition to these issues, there are many other points that are necessary to consider in this analysis to understand those changes such as the interests of Europe and the impacts they had on Moroccan Jews during the 19th century. Moreover, the role of mediator that Moroccan Jews played between European powers and Sharifian government during the 19th century.

Given the importance of these points in understanding the changing Jewish legal status in Morocco, it is necessary first to identify the status of Jews in pre-colonial Morocco. After that it is important to address the growing influence of European powers in North Africa in the nineteenth century, which ultimately led Morocco to come under French protectorate in 1912. Then, to the important reforms that have been introduced during the French protectorate in Morocco. In conclusion, this book mentions the status of Jews in Morocco after independence. To do so, this research is organized into three chapters. The first chapter addresses the development of legal status of Jews in Moroccan Islam through constitutional texts up to modern time. The purpose of this chapter is to address the legitimate and legal origin of Jewish legal status in Morocco. It also presents some details of the concepts contained in *'Ahd* of 'Umar (*al-Shurūt al-'Umarīyah*) and the classical Islamic jurisprudence compared with the modern concepts such as full citizenship to understand how they were applied in Morocco. It also drives the applications of the rules of Islamic legal status in theoretical level to Jewish reality in Morocco. The second chapter looks at the changing of Jewish legal status in Morocco during the 19th century in reality and the attitude of Moroccan government about this change. The purpose of this chapter is to understand how European powers in Morocco contributed to this change. It also addresses factual aspects of the interests of foreign intervention, especially in the Jewish question, and the impacts of the protégé in Morocco during the 19th century. The third chapter presents the ambiguous legal status of Jews during the time of French Protectorate in Morocco 1912 until 1956. The purpose of this chapter is to analyze the Jewish legal status in light of the emergence of Moroccan nationalism in the end of the protectorate. Generally, it also looks at the factors that led Moroccan government to recognize Jews as full citizens.

CHAPTER I

-

The Historical Developments of Jewish Legal Status through Constitutional Texts Up to the 20th Century

Morocco became officially an Islamic country in the 8th century, but Jews have lived in Morocco before the arrival of Islam.[87] In the absence of precise information about the existence of other religious groups before the Islamic conquest, Jews were the only religious minority.[88] Concerning the Andalusian Christians who had been expelled and deported to Morocco in the 12th century, they were living amid of their community and had their own churches.[89] However, those who did not return to Spain in the 14th century integrated completely in the Muslim populations. So, since the 14th century, Jews were only religious minority in Morocco.[90] Morocco was a diverse society, consisting of religious groups and tribes; Berbers and Arabs.

This chapter addresses how the constitutional texts dealt with this diversity; how it is reflected in historical reality between Muslims and Jews in Morocco and to what extent were Moroccan rulers able to respond to

---

[87] Haim Zafrani, *Two Thousands Years of Jewish Life in Morocco*, 1.

[88] Mohammed Kenbib, *Juifs et Musulmans au Maroc, 1859-1948*, 17.

[89] The historical sources indicate that the Caliph of Almoravids "Ali ibn Yusuf b. Tachfin expelled the Christians from the Andalusia and deported them to Morocco in the year 1126 AD. The reason for taking this decision is that the Christians of Granada collaborated with 'Alfonso' to enable him to access to the city. This event had seen as a get out of the *dhimma* requirements though *'Ulama* eyes of that time, especially by Averroes who considered this alienation and deportation as a lighter/less punishment to them. Hence, in the twelfth century there was a group of Christians in Morocco alongside to Muslim and Jews. (Muhammad Ibn 'Idhārī, *Kitāb al-Bayān al-Mughrib fī akhbār al-Andalus wa-al-Maghrib*)

(*محمد ابن عذاري المراكشي، المتوفى 1295 ميلادي، البيان المغرب في أخبار الأندلس والمغرب*)

[Taḥqiq wa-murāja'at G S Colin; Evariste Lévi-Provençal; Iḥsān 'Abbās] (Beirut: Dār al-Thaqāfah, 1983), Volume 4, 72-77.

[90] Muhammad Tahtah, *Brothers Enemies: the Jews of Morocco in the Modern era.* 16 /01/2012. http://www.hespress.com/orbites/45471.html (Accessed 10/28/2015).

these challenges of religious diversity in their society. The purpose is to understand the problems which drove the challenges that emerged in modern history of Morocco to the traditional status of Jews and adoption of new changes in Jewish legal status in Morocco until independence in 1956. To find out this issue, it will be illustrated through two sections. The first section, clarifies concepts such as *Ahl al-Dhimma* and *dhimmis* by drawing a picture on the development of the concept of *Ahl al-Dhimma* in Islamic classical *fiqh*. The second, analyzes the historical development of the consecutive texts that determine the status of Jews in Moroccan Islam.

Clarifying the Concepts.

According to the Islamic teachings, people are divided to two groups. One follows religion of Islam and the other does not.[91] On the basis of this division, the position of a person is determined in political Islamic jurisprudence.[92] For this consideration, the Muslims jurists divided the world into *Dar al-Islam*[93] and *Dar al-Harb*.[94] There is a rule in classical *fiqh*

---

[91] There are several verses in the Quran assert this meaning. One of verses in the Surah 64 is the verse 2 states that Allah says "He it is Who created you, then some of you are disbelievers and some of you are believers. And Allah is All-Seer of what you do". In addition Allah says in the Surah 45 verses 30-31 "Then, as for those who believed (in the Oneness of Allah) and did righteous good deeds, their Lord will admit to His Mercy. That will be the evident success. But as for those who disbelieved (it will be said to them): Were not Our Verses recited to you? But you were proud, and you were a people who were Mujrimun (polytheists, disbelievers, sinners, criminals). These verses clearly indicate that people are two teams. One believes in the message of Islam, which is a Muslim, and another not believes in it, which is non-Muslim.

[92] Abd al- Karim Zaydan, *Ahkam al-Dmmiin wa-al Musta'min fi Dar al-Islam*, 11.

[93] Dar al-Islam is used by classical *fiqh* to describe a Land that is under the rule of Muslims, where Muslim rulers provide a security to people who are living there whether they are Muslim or are not. In contrast, dar al-Harb is used by classical *fiqh* to describe non-Muslim's lands that were under the rule of non-Muslim suggesting that all such lands should be considered as at war until it come under the rule of Muslims. For these classifications see the book by ʻAbd al-Wahhab, Khalaf, *Islamic politics* [al-Siyāsā al-Shar′iya](Cairo: 1932), 69.

which determined the status of Islamic law concerning people living in a Muslim country, whether they are Muslims or not, states that "if Islamic law is a religion and law for Muslims, it is a law for non-Muslims as long as they live in *Dar al-Islam*".[95] It is possible to illustrate the evolution of the legal status of non-Muslims, who were permitted to live in territories of Islam through the study of two terms that emerged in the Islamic jurisprudence; the contracts of *al-Amān* and *al-Dhimma*. Thus, this section will address two fundamental relevant issues; first, the historical development of the legal text to codify the relationship between Jews and Muslims. The second is the role of Muslim jurists in codifying this relationship, but before that, it is necessary first to mention *'Aqd al-Amān*.

The Safety Contract (*'Aqd al-Amān*).

The safety contract (*'Aqd al-Amān*), in classical *fiqh*, is a temporary contract, which regulates the relationship between Islamic State and non-Muslims who want to stay for a limited period in a Muslim country for any legitimate reason such as trade, visiting relatives, treatment and hospitalizations, learning, teaching, tourism or for any other purpose.[96] This contract provides for the owner (*Musta'man*) of it limited rights including the rights to protection and security (assurance of safety) for his life, honor and property and also the right of temporary residence and movement.[97]

---

[94] There is nowhere such classification explicitly in the Quran, and neither was it known in the time of the Prophet or His companions. It was developed by classical *fiqh* later according to their political and social considerations.

[95] Abd al- Karim Zaydan, *Ahkam al-Dmmiin wa-al Musta'min fi Dar al-Islam* (Beirut: Maktbat al-9uds, 1982), 5.

[96] Abd al- Karim Zaydan, *Ahkam al-Dmmiin wa-al Musta'min fi Dar al-Islam*, 46.

[97] Abd al-Rāhmān al-Najdi, *Ahkām 'aqd al-Amān wa-al Musta'min fi al-Islam* (Riyadh: 1990), 105.

According to Maliki *fiqh*, it is not allowed for everyone to hurt *Musta'manin* and not allow to anyone oppress them because they are protected by force of law, which is reflected in this contract. Thus, it must be on the highest of authority in the Muslim state to protect them.[98] Maliki jurists go even further, when they discuss the question if the *Musta'man*'s country asks his extradition. In this sense, Abd al-Rāhmān al-Najdi in his work *Ahkām 'Aqd al-Amān wa-al Musta'man fi al-Islam* states that it is not allowed to extradite *al Musta'man* to his state until the contract has expired even if his state threatens to fight the Muslim state. He points out that classical jurists consider this contract something sacred.[99] Concerning the question of who has the right to issue the safety contract, according to Abd al- Karim Zaydan in his work *Ahkam ahl al-Dhimma wa-al Musta'man fi Dar al-Islam*, Maliki *fiqh* hold that contact is issued by the competent authority with permission of the head of state and does not allow to anyone to issue it.[100] In his comment about Maliki *fiqh* Abd al- Karim Zaydan holds that this is the appropriate *fiqh* to modern time because the *Imam* is a responsible for the interest of the country.[101] In harmonization of the safety contract with the contemporary context and make it fit today's context, it can be argued that it is quite similar to the modern system of a visa in the international relations today.

This contract is not a subject of this research, but the purpose was to clarify the position of non-Muslims living in a Muslim country. Generally, concerning non-Muslim living in Islamic territory, they were divided into

[98] Ibid.
[99] Ibid.
[100] Abd al- Karim Zaydan, *Ahkam al-Dmmiin wa-al Musta'min fi Dar al-Islam*, 49.
[101] Ibid.

two groups. The first one is not indigenous people of a Muslim country, but they come for some reasons such as work. The applicable law for those is the contract safety that studied above because their residence is not permanent. The second is *Ahālī* or non-Muslims who are indigenous people of the state and are living permanently in a Muslim country. The legal status of those is regulated under the contract of *al-Dhimma ('Aqd al-Dhimma*), so they were called *Ahl al-Dhimma*. This contract and these people are the subject of this research and it will be discussed here.

The *Dhimma* Contract *('Aqd al-Dhimma*).

In order to understand the nature of relations between the Muslim state and *Ahl al-Dhimma (Ahl al-Kitāb*) and to clarify the notion of the phrase of *Ahl al-Dhimma*, it is important to get back to the era in which has seen the beginning of implementation of what is known later the *dhimma* law in classical *fiqh*. There were many historical and political circumstances led to the establishment of the legal status of *Ahl al-Dhimma*. Hence, it can be argue that economy, religious, and political considerations, arising during the era of *al-Khulafā al-Rāshidūn* (632 until 661 AD) and after,[102] had significant impacts on the dramatic shift that has taken place on the legal status of *Ahl al-Dhimma*. The effects of these considerations continued its interactions up to the nineteenth century and the first half of twentieth century in which the Islamic legal status was canceled in many Muslim states.

[102] This is a term is used by Sunni Islam to refer to the first four Caliphs who ruled the Muslims after the death of the Prophet Muhammad between 632 and 661 AD.

Clarifying the Concept of *Ahl al-Dhimma and Dhimmis.*

The *dhimmis* were treated under the rule of Islam within the framework of what has been termed *Ahl al-Dhimma*.[103] The term of *Ahl al-Dhimma* was known first in classical jurisprudence to define the people who may be held *'Aqd al-Dhimma* of non-Muslims in a Muslim country.[104] The word *dhimma* as it is specified in the famous Arabic dictionaries and also in Islamic Law and carried on in Moroccan practice means protection. According to the classical dictionary *Lisan al-'Arab,* the term of *dhimma* is derived from the Arabic word "الذمة", literally meaning "covenant, contract *('Aqd),* protection, guarantee, safety, custody, sanctity and duty".[105] *Dhimmis* or *Ahl al-Dhimma* is the name applied by classical Muslim jurists to indigenous non-Muslims from *Ahl al-Kitāb,* and also to who enter under such rule as Zoroastrians (*Majūs*), living in the Islamic territory permanently.[106] Therefore, it is called *dhimmis "Ahl al'Ahd*" (people of the covenant).[107] The term means that they are in custody of Allah and His Messenger and are not in the custody of any one of people.[108] The Qur'an mentions this meaning of the term of *dhimma* twice in Surah 9 (*al-Taubah*) the verses 8 and 10 in the context of speaking about the relationship between Muslims and *mushrikūn* in the case in which *mushrikūn* are the victors. The verses say that "With regard to believer, they respect not the ties, either of kinship or of covenant! It is they who are the transgressors".[109]

---

103 The *dhimmis* were known as *Ahl al-Kitāb, Ahl al-Dhimma,* or protected people.
104 Magdy Girgis, *Coptic Judiciary in Egyp*t [al-Qdha al-Qabti], (Cairo: 1999), 5.
105 Muhammad Ibn Manzur, *Lisan al-'Arab* [the Arab tongue](Beirut, 1990) Volume, 15/ 111.
106 Muhammad ibn Abu Bakr ibn Qayyim al-Jawziyyah, *Ahkam Ahl al-Dhimma*, 78.
107 Abd al-Wahab El-Messiri, *Jews, Judaism and Zionism encyclopedia*. Volume 4/325.
108 Ibid.
109 (لايرقبون في مومن إلا ولاذمة، وأولئك هم المعتدون. الاية،8)

The word *dhimma* in these verses is used in the meaning of *'ahd* (convenant).

The Stability of this Term in Islamic Jurisprudence to Refer to non-Muslims.

Tracking the root of the term and its origin and how it became steady in Islamic jurisprudence to refer to non-Muslim who living in a Muslim territory permanently. In the Qur'an, there is no use of this expression to refer to non-Muslims. However, the Qur'an used other expressions to refer to nom-Muslims such as *Ahl al-Kitāb*, *al-Nasārā wa al-Yahud*, pagans and infidels.[110] Regarding *Hadiths*, the Prophet of Islam used this expression to indicate the non-Muslims of Muslim territories. Thus, the expression idiomatically appeared in Islam with the Prophet use of this term in his many sayings (*hadiths)*, such as "Whoever hurt a *dhimmi* has hurt me, and I will dispute with him on the Day of Judgment" ("من أذى ذميا فقد أذاني وأنا خصمه يوم القيامة").[111] And also in farewell speech (*Jabal 'Arafat*), "I command you to deal with *Ahl al-Dhimma* well (to do the good with them because they are in my custody)" ("أوصيكم بأهل ذمتي خيراً").[112] Through this descriptive formula that was used by the Prophet in these *Hadiths*, the term of *Ahl al-Dhimma* became a vocabulary in Arab communication to address non-Muslims whether in practice, or in the books of *fiqh*. However, although the expression of *"dhimma"* was used by the Prophet and in his treaties, it was a vocabulary that was used in the speech of Arabs before Islam, where the

[110] Ibid.

[111] Reported by Al-Khatib with authentic chain of narrations and also by At -Tabarani in *Al-Awsat* with good chain of narrators.

[112] Abd al-Wahab El-Messiri, *Jews, Judaism and Zionism encyclopedia*, V.4/325.

protection and the care of neighborhood were one of the key personal attributes and the requirements of magnanimity in Arab community.[113] Thus, the status of *dhimma* was a case of treaty that was known to Arabs before Islam (*jahiliyyah*). Then, at a later stage, the expression developed during the classical period of Islamic jurists and thus, *'Aqd al-Dhimma* became a synonym for the term *al-Shurūt al-'Umarīyah*.[114] Consequently, it stabilized in the Islamic idiosyncratic and legal construction and served as a terminology to refer to non-Muslims in a Muslim community and also in the legal elaboration of Jewish status in Islamic territories. This led to talk about the foundational texts to the legal status of Jews to know the history of the real start of the implementation of the *dhimma* system.

Jewish Legal Status and Islamic Legal Heritage.

The *dhimma* system drives most its characteristic form from a document known as *al-Shurūt al-'Umariyya*, "a kind of bilateral contract in which non-Muslims agree to a host of discriminatory regulations in return for protection".[115]

The Establishment of the System in the Time of the Prophet.

The basic center of the call that was launched by the Prophet of Islam was a theistic attempt in which, on the one hand, it has focused on the argument of the belief in one God as creator of the universe. On the other hand, it has focused on the principle of the equality of human beings and

---

[113] Magdy Girgis, *Coptic Judiciary in Egypt*, 5

[114] Ibid.

[115] Mark R. Cohen, *Under Crescent and Cross: the Jews in the Middle Ages* (New Jersey: 1994), 54.

their responsibilities before God at the Judgment Day.[116] Through these principles, the Prophet faced a great hostility from the Quraysh of Mecca. So, on that basis, he felt that he was close to the Jews because they shared the same perspective about these principles.[117] During his time in Mecca before his migration to Medina, the principle of the belief of the revelation of the book was only a criterion that divided people to two different categories; idolaters that were called (*mushrikūn*) and monotheistic (*mua'minūn*) including Muslim, Jews and Christians.[118] In this regard, when the Prophet was forced to move to Medina, the population of Medina was a mix of many different tribes, especially of Jews.[119] He immediately became founder of religious-political community, so he rapidly started combining all communities that were living there to form one community, which is he called *Ummah*.[120] In this respect, he held a public treaty with Muslims on one hand and with Jews on the other. This public treaty is known as a Constitution of Medina or in Arabic *Ṣaḥīfat al-Madīna*.[121] The principal motive that encouraged the Prophet to do so is that he was believed that the theistic experiment is a way of rapprochement with the Jews of Medina to fight against the Quraysh of Mecca and also as pillar of building a new society as one community.[122] The purpose of the Prophet was to establish a

---

116 Hassān al-Zayn, *al-Awdā' al-Qānuniyya,* 6.

117 Ibid.

118 ibid

119 The historical sources report that Medina was filled with Jews belonging to several tribes, when the Prophet came to there. In addition, it was strong relations between Jews and Arab tribes such as Khazraj and Aws until those become familiar with the Jewish ideas. See, for example, Hassan Ibrahim Hassan, *Tarikh al-Islam*, V. 1 (Beirut: Dar al-Jil, 1991), 79.

120 See the document of Medina in the book *Muhammad Rasul Alla*h by Muhammad Reda (Beirut: 2006), 157-159.

121 And this time Medina became consisting three groups: Immigrants, supporters and Jews. See, Hassan Ibrahim Hassan, *Tarikh al-Islam*, V. 1, 85.

122 Hassan Ibrahim Hassan, *Tarikh al-Islam*, V. 1, 88.

new society and put the rules of an Islamic state based primarily on the concept of ummah, which has a political and civil nature and also on unifying not based on religion, dogma, or tribe.[123] *Saḥīfat al-Madīna* contains many principles of new community regulations and organizations. Among these principles that are related to this section's argument are the statements about the position of Jews in Medina in this new community. It was stated in clause 25 that "The Jews of Banu Awf (non-Muslim minorities) shall be considered one community along with the Muslims, and they have their religion and the Muslims have their religion except those behave unjustly and sinfully",[124] and in clauses 1 and 2, it was stated that "the believers and the Muslims of the Quraysh and Yathrib and those who shall follow them and fight along with them are/form one community/nation".[125] It was also stated in clause 20 that "the Jews shaped one community along with the believers and the Jews who follow us have the right to receive help and assistance from Muslims as long as they (Jews) do not work against the Muslims or provide aid to the enemies of the Muslims".[126] *Saḥīfat al-Madina* identified the members who composed what was termed one nation/community, which are believers of the new religion and who follow and join them and fight with them such as Bedouins, hypocrites and Jews. The first clause states that this document applies to its original parties and who follow them without specification of a group over the other. This principle is repeated again in the clause 16 pointing to the Jews in

---

[123] Ahmed Sha'ibi, "Document of Medina: the Content and Significance", published by *the nation book*, volume 110, 2006, 87.

[124] Ibid.,44.

[125] Ibid.,41.

[126] Muhammad Tahir-ul-Qadr, *The Constitution of Medina: 63 Constitutional Articles*, (London: Minhaj-ul-Quran Publications, 2012), 7.

particular. It was stated that "the Jews who follow us have the same right of protection and also the right to receive help and assistance from us (state)".[127] *Saḥīfat al-Madina* shows that the political community, which was created by the Prophet, was a contractual community and varied in religious affiliation. *Al-Saḥīfat* is not only announced that all tribes in Yathrib are one community, but it explicitly declared that the Jews form one community with believers in the clauses from 25 until 35.[128] Therefore, the Jews formed with Muslims a community in a political sense and not in a religious sense. In this sense, this new community was an ummah in a political sense and two ummah in a religious sense. In addition to that the clauses of *al-Saḥīfat* did not prevent Jews from participating in the defense of the state in case of an attack on the state. It was stated in the clause 54, "The Muslims and the Jews shall be jointly responsible to defend (the state of) Madina against any outside attack".[129] On this basis, *Saḥīfat al-Madina* is the first constitutional text that set up the basic guidelines of the relationship between Jews and Muslims in one community. It was able to combine all communities that were in Yathrib according to a new vision based mainly on the concept of ummah in a political sense not in a religious sense. However, these principles were not respected by some Jews of Yathrib, where it was appeared the first attempts of the violations of the contents of *al-Saḥīfat* in the aftermath of the Battle of Badr.

Following the Battle of Badr[130] it appeared some members of the Jews of Medina indicated a lack of commitment, and thus an end of the agreement

[127] Ahmed Sha'ibi, *Document of Medina*, 43.
[128] Ibid,.88.
[129] Muhammad Tahir-ul-Qadr,*The Constitution of Medina*, 15.
[130] This Battle was in 624 AD as the first military war between Muslims and Quraysh.

with them. They set up a secret relationship with the Quraysh to kill the Prophet Mohammad.[131] The plot hatched by the Jews of Qaynuqa' in collaboration with the Quraysh created a kind of caution and suspicion among Muslims.[132] The plot was obvious when the Prophet went to their neighborhood and told them that 'he is the messenger of Allah and the Jews know this'. They responded to him by saying that 'we are unlike the Quraysh, who do not have an experience in fighting in war, and we are experts in fighting'.[133] Given that the majority of this Jewish tribe were goldsmiths and blacksmiths, they were more dangerous and subject to doubt in the eye of the Muslims of Medina. Due to this consideration, this tribe received the first blow were forced to leave Medina.[134] Shortly afterwards, other Jewish tribes also did not adhered with the terms of treaty such as the tribes of Nazir and Qurayza.[135] This was followed by a series of events starting with the defeat of Muslim military in the battle of *Uhud*, and ending with the battle of Khaybar, which was a victory of Muslim military in the year 6 Hijri.[136] In the aftermath of battle of Khaybar, the Prophet returned all synagogues to the Jews in Khaybar and did not force them to convert to Islam. So, it has been a new attempt to establish a unity

---

[131] Wasfi al-Rahman Mubaarakfoori, *Sealed Nectar in the Prophet's Biography* (Qatar: 2007), 238.

صفي الرحمن المباركفوري ، الرحيق المختوم في سيرة الرسول

[132] Hassān al-Zayn, *al-Awdā' al-Qānuniyya*, 9.

[133] Israel Welfensohn said that Jews answered the Prophet boldly and vaunt. *History of Jews in Arab countries* [*Tarikh al-Yahud fi bilad al-Aarb fi al-Jahiliyyah wa Sadri al-Islam*] (Cairo: 1927), 129.

[134] Ibid.

[135] The battle of Nazir was in 625 AD and the battle of Qurayza was in 627 AD. To see details about those battles and its reasons see the book *Muhammad Rasul Allah* by Muhammad Reda, 242-267.

[136] Hassān al-Zayn, al-Awdā' al-Qānuniyya, 9.

administration with Jews, but it did not succeed.[137] In the mildest of these events, one realizes that the system of Medina was stillborn, where emerged a new relation with Jews. Therefore, all future relations between Islam and Monotheistic religions were affected by this big clash between Jews and Muslims in Madina. In the mildest of these tensions that began floating on the relationship between the Jews and the Prophet, the Qur'an begins to reconsider this relationship, especially between Jews who broke the covenants. Among these verses the verse 82 in Surah 5 (*al-Maidah)*. Allah said "Verily, you will find the strongest among men in enmity to the believers (Muslims) the Jews and those who are pagans". This situation led to a political crisis that began increasing day by day. The Prophet felt that he was unsuccessful in his mission, which aimed to unite the Jews and Arabs and to find a nation composed of all groups in Yathrib. However, in spite of that, the Prophet did not change his dealing with Jews. Among examples that show these is his dealing with the Jews of Khaybar, where he returned all their synagogues and did not force them to convert to Islam, but he signed with them a covenant of peace in 628 AD.[138] Hence, these events led in the end to bring about a change in the constitutive text of legal status of Jews. There is a verse determining a new status for Jews. In the verse 29 in Surah 9 (*al-Taubah)*, Allah said: "Fight against those who believe not in Allah, nor in the last day, nor forbid that which has been forbidden by Allah and His Messenger and those who acknowledge not the religion of truth among the people of the Scripture, until they pay the *jiziyah* with willing submission, and feel themselves subdued". This verse was a significant turning point in

[137] Ibid.

[138] Ibid., and also the book of *History of Jews in Arab countries* by Israel Welfensohn, 157-174.

the legal status of Jews in the first era of Islam. It provides new procedures towards the status of Jews, where it was adding the *jiziyah*. It was the first practical application of this procedure with the Christians of Najran in 631 AD.[139] In fact, those texts genuinely reflect the early Islamic attitude towards Jews. It is appropriate to quote here Mark R. Cohen who summarizes the situation of Jews with the Prophet. Cohen points out that

> Muhammad established another precedent for religious toleration in the Constitution of Medina, his compact with the Arabs and some of the Jews of Medina, which granted the Jews autonomy to the latter. True, Muhammad later fiercely repressed the Jews in reaction to their enmity and ridicule, but this kind of conduct was not the norm in Muhammad's treatment of non-Muslims. His treaties with the Jewish or Christian inhabitants of various other oases and towns in Arabia guaranteed them safety in return of tribute, a policy that endured.[140]

These new relations will be organized in independent treaties that will take later the name of the contract of *al-Dhimma* or the contract of *al-Sulh* (reconciliation). These contracts contain various clauses of the legal bases for a kind of communal independence for the so-called later *Ahl al-Dhimma*. All the contracts that were signed by the Prophet with the Jews and

[139] The books of Prophet's biography tell us about Najran delegation. This delegation came to prophet in Medina in the context of response to a letter sent by him inviting them to Islam. After a long conversation between them and the Prophet about his message and also about his opinion about Jesus, they refused to accept Islam. Thus, they wanted a peace treaty, promising to accept all what they agreed on. They signed a peace agreement in return of paying *jiziyah*.
صفي الرحمن المباركفوري ، *الرحيق المختوم في سيرة الرسول*، 450-51.

[140] Mark R. Cohen, *Under Crescent and Cross,* 55.

Christian (the famous one is Najran treaty in the year 10 Hijri -631AD) and also the letters that were sent to them reflected this new legal status. Therefore, it has emerged the foundations of *'Aqd al-Dhimma* and set up in the time of the Prophet. All the Jews and Christians subjected to this *'Aqd* are called *Ahl al-Dhimma* and *al-Dhimmis.*

The System of *Dhimma* and the Big Change.

The system of *dhimma* established in the Prophet's time, where it was to a large extent a product of peace treaties and letters which the Prophet signed or sent to inhabitants of areas that were conquered or made peace with him. These treaties and letters led, in the end, to the emergence of the expression of *'Aqd* or *Ahd al Dhimma.*[141] However, following the time of the Prophet, the series of many political considerations played a big role in bringing about change in the *dhimma* system and push it in a new different trend during the first periods of the Islamic conquests.[142] This shift in the legal *dhimma* system peaked which caused the emergence the so-called *'ahd* 'Umar or al-*Shurūt al-'Umarīyah* (stipulations of *'Umar*), where it imposes on *dhimmis* a case of hostility and ill-treatment.[143] Legally, the difference between the contents of *al-Shurūt al-'Umarīyah* and the peace treaties in the time of the Prophet and his successors clearly explains the strength of the change. The tone of contempt and various abuses that were used in *al-Shurūt al-'Umarīyah* indicate to a fundamental change in the legal status of *Ahl al-Dhimma.*[144] This document, legally, served as a key foundational text

141 Hassān al-Zayn, *al-Awdā' al-Qānuniyya*, 284.
142 Ibid.
143 Ibid.,22.
144 Ibid., 284.

in the legal formulation of *dhimmis* status during the period of Islamic classical *fiqh* and, in practice, as a main source of any arbitrary actions towards *Ahl al-Dhimma* whenever there are political reasons calling for it. These conditions, which a number of researchers[145]see that, were decided in the 'Abbasid reign[146] and were attributed to the Caliph 'Umar to take a legal force.

The Origin of the *al-Shurūt al-'Umarīyah.*

It is important to start by quoting here Professor Cohen in his describing *al-Shurūt al-'Umariyya*. He states that *al-Shurūt al-'Umariyya* is "itself a product of cumulative development based on Muhammad's practice, the exigencies of [Arab] conquests, and the influence of Christian-Roman Jewry Law".[147] The professor Hassan al-Zayn states a set of factors that led to the emergence of *al-Shurūt al-'Umariyya* in its final form in classical Islamic Jurisprudence.[148] It is also important to bring here two versions of the pact of 'Umar; one exists in the historians and traditions sources and another is in the classical jurisprudence. Through following the track of this document in medieval classical Islamic writings, it has been found that there are two main dates in the development of this document, and also there are two versions of this document which vary in its content. With respect to the historical books, the first Muslim historian who reported the pact of 'Umar is Ya'qubi (284 AH, 898 A.D) in his book *History*[149]in a brief formula about 250 years of the date of *'uhda al-'Umarīyah*/the pact of 'Umar (15 AH). Then

145 Mark R. Cohen, Hassan al-Zin, Abd al-Rahman Kahila
146 Ibid.
147 Mark b. Cohen, *Under Crescent and Cross*, 57.
148 Hassan al-Zayn, *al-Awdā' al-Qānuniyya*, 11-26.
149 Ya'coubi, *The history of Ya'coubi* (Beirut: 2010), 37.

he was followed by several historians such as al-Tabari. From a historical perspective, the text of al-Tabari is considered the longest and the best one among versions in the historian sources.[150] The Document, in the version as exists in historical books, is a written charter by 'Umar b. al-Khattāb to people of Jerusalem for a guaranteed of protection and allows them to practice their religions freely. In this version, there is no mention of any derogatory conditions and restrictions, especially certain conditions, as will appear later in the version of the Islamic jurists and also there is no mentioning to *jiziyah.*[151] The version do exist in *Hadiths* sources is similar to the historian sources; especially they earmark a significant part to the provisions of *dhimmis* such as Ibn Hibban (965 A.D)[152], in his book الثقات (Trustworthy), and Ibn 'Asākir (1177 A.D) in his book *History of Damascus.*[153]

Unlike the historian and tradition sources, the medieval Islamic jurisprudence sources refer to a different version of *'Uhdah al-'Umarīyah.* They narrate a written answer to *al-'Uhdah al-'Umarīyah* (in particular the letter from the Christians Jerusalem to 'Umar) under the name of *al-Shurūt al-'Umarīyah.* Concerning the first jurisprudential sources that report this document, according to, an Egyptian researcher Abd al-Rahman, the first time when this version was appeared in jurisprudential sources was in the second half of the third century AH, 864 AD,[154] in particular, in the book

150 Ramadan Isaac Azayan "'Umar's pact Narratives: Documental Study", *Journal of the Islamic University* (Islamic Studies Series) Volume XIV, issue 2 (June: 2006)185.

151 See the text in *the History of Ya'coubi*, 37.

152 Muhammad Ibn Hibban, الثقات *(Trustworthy)* (The Ministry of Knowledge high for the government of India: 1978), 213.

153 Ramadan Isaac Azayan *'Umar's pact Narratives*, 176.

154 Abd al-Rahman Kahila, *The Covenant of Umar: A New Reading* (Cairo: 1996), 55.

Ahkam Ahl al-Milal by al-Khallal Abi Bakr Ahmed al-Baghdadi al-Hanbali (311 AH, 935 AD). Then was followed in the second half of the fourth century Hijri, by another book by Abi al-Shaykh (369 HA, 941 AD) under title *Shurūt 'Umar"* or *Shurūt al-Dhimmis.*[155] After that *al-Shurūt al-'Umarīyah* became famous among Classical jurists. Among jurists who dealt directly with *al-Shurūt al-'Umarīyah* Abi al-Qasim al-Tabari (418 AH, 1019 AD) in his works entitled *the Explanation of the Kitāb of 'Umar.* In addition, in the year 458 Hijri, there was another book entitled *Shurūt Ahl al-Dhimma* of al-Qadi Abi Ya'la (458AH, 1066 AD).[156] Since the most of these books are still in manuscript and not print, the oldest printed book that contains *al-Shurūt al-'Umarīyah* is the book of the Andalusian jurist Ibn Hazm (456 AH, d 1064) in his *Kitāb al-Muhallā.*[157] Thus, Ibn Qayyim al-Jawziyyah (d. 1350), is not considered to be the first one who state this document in his book *Ahkam ahl al-Dhimma* because he quoted and based his work on other books in gathering his data.

With respect to the application of *al-Shurūt al-'Umarīyah,* it goes back to the year 700 AH, 1302 AD, where was mentioned officially and practically to *al- Shurūt al-'Umarīyah* and the reference to this *al-Shurūt* became usual thing by states and was applied.[158] In this context, under title "Confirmation of the convenant to *dhimmis*", Abd al-Rahman Ibn Khaldūn, in his book known as *Tarikh Ibn Khaldūn* reports a story showing that the first time it was mentioned officially and practically to *al- Shurūt al-'Umarīyah* was in a meeting consists of religious *'Ulama,* the Christian Patriarch and the head of

[155] Ibid.,56.
[156] Ibid.,57.
[157] Ibid.,58.
[158] Ibis., 61.

Jewish community and also a group of *dhimmis*, which was convened by the Sultan al-Nasir Muhammad b. Qalwun in Egypt, in 1301.[159] According to Kahilah what happened in this year was repeated again in subsequent years in which it sometimes was accompanied by the demolition of the churches.[160] However, one it may argue that what was happening sometimes of persecution or semi persecution was the exception not a rule, which it associated with a specific events and historical context.

In terms of content, this document addresses the rules that regulate the relationship between *dhimmis* and Muslim state in addition to that all these rules are in favor of Muslims and inconsistent with what was the situation in the previous covenants. Generally, it states the conditions and restrictions that *al-Dhimmis* should follow towards Islam and Muslims. Thus, *al-Shurūt al-'Umarīyah* centers around the stipulations which the Christians of Jerusalem imposed on themselves. It addresses the stipulations in a formal letter to 'Umar b. al-Khattāb requesting from him "a guarantee security for adherence to a set of seemingly humiliating conditions"[161] such as "not to build in their cities or in their vicinity new churches, hermitages, monasteries, or monk's cells, not to renew the churches that have fallen into

[159] The story tells that, in the year 1301, when a vizier from *al-Maghreb*, in his way to *al-Haj*, arrived to Egypt and saw the status of *dhimmis* and on what they are of luxury and what they have achieved of senior positions in Egypt, he outraged at this status of local *dhimmis* and condemn what he saw. This strong reaction of vizier toward the status of *dhimmis* in Egypt put the Sultan in an embarrassing position. Thus he ordered to convene a meeting attended by religious representatives of three monotheistic faiths. They discussed the status of *dhimmis* in light of the pervious Muslim treaties, where in the end they agreed on a set of restrictions that reported in *al- Shurūt al-'Umarīyah*. On behalf of their communities, the heads of Jews and Christian committed themselves to adhere to the contents of this document and not violate that. It was sent this agreement to all Egyptian and Levantine states to apply all restrictions of *al- Shurūt al-'Umarīyah* without exception. Ibn Khaldūn (d. 1406), *Kitāb al-'ibar* [Tarikh ibn Khaldūn] (Beirut: Dar al-Fikr, 2000), 476-77.

[160] Abd al-Rahman Kahila, *the Covenant of Umar*, 62.

[161] Mark b. Cohen, "What was the Pact of 'Umar? Literally Historical Studies", *JSAI* 23 (1999), 103.

ruin or which are located in the quarters of Muslims and adhering their dress such as binding *the zunnār(*a distinctive belt*)* around their waists and not to teach their children the Qur'an".[162] After The Caliph 'Umar b. al-Khattāb received this letter, he wrote to 'Abd al-Rahmān B. Ghanm commanding him to sign what they asked with the addition of the two amendments. "They shall not buy anyone made prisoner by the Muslims", and "whoever strikes a Muslim which deliberate intent shall forfeit the protection of this pact".[163] 'Abd al-Rahmān b. Ghanm implemented 'Umar's recommendation and applied these conditions also to the Christians of Jerusalem and of all the cities in the Levant.[164] The reason that led Medieval Islamic jurisprudence to adopt this document and based on in the field of codifying the relationship between the Islamic state and non-Muslim citizens were the political considerations in their time. To find solutions for these problems, as Kahila points out, their conscientiousness led them to decide rules unreasonable unjustifiable.[165] Thus, it has shown that the document is only a result of the diligence of jurists who attributed it to 'Umar b. Khattāb to take a legal force. On the other hand, generally, jurisprudence is only a human action that is subjected to the reality factors in which it is influenced by economic, political, social considerations and therefore is not obligated for all followed ages as *al-Shurūt al-'Umarīyah.*

162 Ibid.,107.
163 Ibid.,108.
164 Ibn Qayyim al-Jawziyyah, *Ahkam Ahl al-Dhimma*, 1109.
165 Abd al-Rahman Kahila, *the Covenant of Umar*, 63.

The Changing Status of *Ahl al-dhimma* in the Islamic Contemporary Texts.

As mentioned above, the development of the *dhimma* system was not only a product of religious considerations. But it was caused by certain circumstances related to intellectual and political conflict at that time; sometimes with the Byzantines and sometimes with Crusaders.[166] Based on this idea, today, especially with the emergence of the concept of liberal citizenship, it "raised many problems by critics of the *dhimma* system, notably the unequal rights and duties it grants Muslims and non-Muslims".[167] This helped several Muslim jurists and intellectuals in attempting to rethink in classical *dhimma* law and to rewrite a new *fiqh* that deals with the issue of *Ahl al-Dhimma* in today's context. They discussed many concepts, which do exist in classical *fiqh* such as the concept of *Ahl al-Dhimma*, citizenship, *jiziyah* and also the pact of 'Umar which forms the basis of the *dhimma* system for jurists. Thus, they have "advanced the concept of *"muwāṭana"* as an authentically Islamic solution to the problems".[168] Their attempting is based on a new reading of the Constitution of Medina *(Saḥīfat al-Madīna)* ratified between the Prophet and non-Muslims in the first year of Hijra "as a potential framework for managing a heterogeneous society, in spite of its apparent abrogation under the rules of traditional jurisprudence".[169] When many of Muslim thinkers (al-Qaradawi, Fahmi Howeidi, Salim al-'Aawa, Rashid Ghannoushi) examined the contents of Document of Medina, they found that the people of

[166] Hassān al-Zayn, *al-Awdā' al-Qānuniyya*, 22.

[167] David H. Warren and Christine Gilmore, "Rethinking neo-Salafism through an Emerging Fiqh of Citizenship: The Changing Status of Minorities in the Discourse of Yusuf al-Qaradawi and the 'School of the Middle Way'", *New Middle Eastern Studies*, issue 2, (29 October 2012), 2.

[168] Ibid.

[169] Ibid.,1.

book were enjoyed the rights of full citizenship in accordance with the Document of Medina. They were also practicing their worship freely, providing advice to the Muslims, and cooperating with them to protect their state from harm and danger, each in his position to carry burdens.[170] Based on this, the concept of *dhimma* is not inconsistent with the concept of citizenship. This was confirmed by Rashid Ghannouchi who said that citizenship is above all differences of national, gender, and language and other differences that established between humans. He also confirmed that the principle of equality of citizens in Islamic state is fixed, when the rights and duties of Muslim do not differ from rights of non-Muslims except in relation to creed. In the same direction, Fahmi Howiedi went on by providing several evidences for his claim which among them in the document of Medina. [171] For Wahba al-Zhili, the citizenship required in Islam the availability of two basics, first: the freedom and the lack of the tyranny of ruler, the second is the availability of equality between citizens in rights and duties regardless of religion, creed or custom.[172] For Ahmed al-Sha'ibi in his book *The Document of Medina*, "the basis of citizenship for non-Muslims is loyalty to Islamic state through the convenant, because the right of citizenship does not require the unity of faith or creed or the unity of race and this corresponds to the clauses of the document of Madina.[173] Based on the concept of liberal citizenship, modern scholars criticize other concepts in the *dhimma* system as the concepts of *al-Dhimma* and *jiziyah.* For al-

[170] Abd al-Wahab El-Messiri, *Jews, Judaism and Zionism encyclopedia*, volume 4/329.

[171] Fahmi Howeidi, *Citizens not Dhimmis* (Cairo: Dar al-Shuru9, 1999), 110.

[172] Wahba al-Zhili, The Concept of Citizenship in the Islamic Perspective, *Islamiyat*, http://www.islameiat.com/Pages/Subjects/Default.aspx?id=15181&cat_id=107. 2 October 2012. Accessed 11/3/2014.

[173] Ahmed al-Sha'ibi, 'Document of Medina: the Content and Significance', 68.

Qaradawi the concept of *al-Dhimma* is not important. In his article written in 1955, *"the rights of non-Muslim minority"*, he argues that there is no need to adhere to the concept *Ahl al-Dhimma* that harm Christians brothers in Egypt and in the Arab and Muslim countries, who mingle with Muslims. He justifies that it is not of pillars of Islam that God obligate us to worship Him through it and 'Umar b. Khattāb deleted the word *jiziyah* although it is mentioned in the Qur'an.[174] However, in another article of al-Qaradawi *the Nation and National-Belonging in the Light of Doctrinal Foundations and the Purposes of Sharia'*, he "went one step farther by shifting away from the *dhimma* model towards a regime of equal citizenship".[175] In addition, and based on reading the Document of Medina, he "appears to suggest that the *dhimma* contract refers to a very different kind of political settlement from the Constitution of Medina and is therefore not a model to be copied in a modern, heterogeneous nation state.[176] This is not only an attitude of Sunni jurisprudence but there is the same attitude of Shi'i jurisprudence. One of them is the Lebanese *Faqih*, Shams al-Din Muhammad Mahdi. With the publication, in 1996, of the *Islamic-Christian dialogue about a project for joint struggle*, he stopped with the concept of *Ahl Al-dhimma* in his book. He criticizes Islamic jurisprudence attributing this Islamic jurisprudential accumulation on the subject of *dhimmis* to a historical matter as a part of historical conditions that no longer exist; claiming to get rid of the obligations and provisions of the jurisprudential outlook towards *dhimmis*

[174] Shaykh Yusuf al-Qaradawi," the Rights of non-Muslim Minority", *the Journal of al-Tawhid*, issue 84, 1955.

[175] David H. Warren and Christine Gilmore, "Rethinking neo-Salafism", 5.

[176] Ibid.

within the concept of *dhimmis*.[177] He also blamed Muslim rulers for the abuses they have done in the context of the application of Islamic law towards *dhimmis*.[178] Fahmi Howiedi suggests that the concept of *Ahl al-Dhimma* become now more descriptions need to be reviewed and revised.[179] In another point, Muhammad al-Ghazali (d.1996) in his book *Intolerance and Tolerance between Christianity and Islam*, denies the existence of *al-Shurūt al-'Umarīyah* arguing that he searched on the origin of these *al-Shurūt* in historical, biography and Islamic books, but he did not find it at all and says that it is bogus and forged.[180] This is also the case for Kahila who threw the responsibility on scholars in creating this *al-Shurūt*.[181] Through this attempt at reading of the Islamic contemporary jurisprudential attitude across a range of contemporary books, it is clear that there is a new change in the legal status of *dhimmis*. This is big evidence that indicates that *fiqh* has nothing to do with religious factors, but it is product of reality when it is born. As for what Jews have suffered from insults and humiliation in Islamic states because of *dhimma*, there is no responsibility for this in Islam, but the scholars and rulers who are the responsible for this.

177Muhammad Mahdi Shams al-Din, *the Islamic-Christian Dialogue: about a Project for Joint Struggle*, (Beirut:2004), 57. http://www.almaaref.org/books/contentsimages/books/dirasat/al_muwatana/page/lesson4.htm.

178 Ibid.

179 Fahmi Howeidi, *Citizens not Dhimmis* , 110

180 Muhammad al-Ghzali, *Intolerance and tolerance between Christianity and Islam* (Cairo: 2000), 45.

181 Abd al-Rahman Kahilah, *the Pact of 'Umar*, 53.

Conclusion

The aim of this chapter was to explore the question of the historical development of constitutional text of the Jewish legal status in Islam from the beginning of the call of the Prophet up to the modern time. It covers the history of the emergence of the first foundational texts that played a significant role in the establishment of the legal status of Jews. First, the Document of Medina that known in Arabic *(Saḥīfat al-Madīna)*, and the second is what is called *al-Shurūt al-'Umarīyah*. Through the chapter, it became clear that this legal status was established in the reign of the Prophet and the constitutional text in the beginning tried to create an integrated society composing of religious groups, races and tribes. Because the Jews were composed a large proportion of the population in Medina, this text considered them indigenous citizens in which they was forming one nation with Muslims. This chapter also illustrates how the status was changed after the emergence of several political factors between Jews and Muslims that led to come down the first verse imposing *jiziyah*, which the first application of it with Najran Christians in 631 AD. Following the death of Prophet, the chapter mentions to some factors that led to emerge the second constitutional text (the pact of 'Umar) that Islamic jurisprudence based on in codifying the legal status of Jews. The chapter discussed the version showing the differences of the contents of these versions in Islamic legal heritage arguing that this text is only a result of the diligence (*ijtihad*) of jurists who attributed it to 'Umar b. Khattāb to take a legal force. For the contemporary *fiqh*, this chapter shows the attempts of modern scholars to create a new understanding to the *dhimma* system by referring to the

Document of Medina as a model of dealing with the heterogeneity and diversity does exist in Muslim communities.

CHPTER II

-

The Legal Emancipation in the Jews' Status in the Mid-19th Century Morocco

The nineteenth century, especially during the second half, is clearly noted by a number of researches,[182] as a turning point in the legal status of Jews in Morocco. In considering the question of legal change in Moroccan Jews' status, one should keep in mind that the influences of European intervention in the internal political and social affairs of Morocco in the mid-19th century played a significant role in this change. Thus, to understand the role of the European intervention in the question of legal change of Jews' status in Morocco, it is necessary to consider, as Muhammad Kenbib points out in his work on Moroccan Jewish-Muslim relations, "that one needs to take into consideration specific historical factors such as power struggles of western powers, economic interests, and relations between Morocco and Europe"[183] on one hand and the general situation of the Jewish communities in this time on the other. Accordingly, this chapter explores how the foreign factors contributed greatly to the legal change of status for Jews in Morocco during the second half of the nineteenth century.

[182] Jessica Marglin, 'Aspects de la modernité judiciaire au Maroc : protégés juifs, tribunaux consulaires et loi islamique', *La bienvenue et l'adieu Migrants juifs et musulmans au Maghreb (XVe-XXe siècle)*, Vo. 1, 2010, 168.

[183] Sharon Vance, "The Martyrdom of a Moroccan Jewish Saint", *Brill's Series in Jewish Studies*, V. 44, 2011, 47.

The legal Status of Jews in the 19th Century.

By the beginning of the 19th century Jews constituted about 7 percent of the population of Morocco, [184] "where they were employed in crafts and trades."[185] According to Muhammad Mansour, "by 1806, their total number was estimated at more than 100,000."[186]Although that most of them moved to live in the main cities, some "continued to live in the most remote areas"[187] such as Tafilelt, Dara 'a valley, Wadi Noun.[188] Many of them "were important merchants residing in the ports and conducting large-scale trade with European countries."[189] Legally, until the turn of the 20th century, Jews "were tied down to *dhimma* status, according to which they were compelled to wear distinctive clothing and to pay *jiziyah*."[190] For instance, in 1843, the Jews of Salé paid *jiziyah* that for three years to the governor of Salé Ahmed 'Aawad.[191] Although Jews, who obtained foreign protection, began to challenge this status by the wearing of European dress, the sultan, as a religious and political leader, had no intention of giving up the applications of the *Dhimma* law on Jews. In 1842, Mawlay 'Abd al-Rahman (1822-1859) mentioned the *al-Shurūt al-'Umarīyah* in "a letter addressed to the French representative in Tangier."[192] Charon Vance quotes this letter referring to Germain Ayache as follows:

---

[184] Turki Ajlan Al-Harithi, "the Changing status of Jews in Morocco in the nineteenth century and the attitude of the Moroccan government", *Historical Studies Journal*, Issues: 45,46, 1993, 188.

[185] Mohamed El Mansour, *Morocco in the reign of Mawaly Sulayman*, 14.

[186] Ibid.

[187] Turki Ajlan Al-Harithi, "the Changing status of Jews in Morocco", 188.

[188] Mohamed El Mansour, *Morocco in the reign of Mawaly Sulayman*, 14.

[189] Ibid.

[190] Ibid.

[191] Turki Ajlan Al-Harithi," the Changing status of Jews in Morocco",189.

[192] Sharon Vance, "The Martyrdom of a Moroccan Jewish Saint", 47

> The Jews, in my states, are bound by the clauses of the contract that applies to protected subjects. These clauses are written in our good law and regulate today, as in the past, the manner in which they are treated by people of our faith. As long as the protégés conform to the clauses under which they are submitted, we are beholden by our law to protect their life and safeguard their property. But if they violate even one of these clauses, the law [of protection] no longer applies to their lives or to their property. Therefore, our religion does not accept from them [anything] except their humility and submission, even to the point that if one of them raises his voice towards a Muslim, it is an infraction.[193]

This attitude also reflected in letters and speeches of the followed Sultan Mawaly Hassan I. He often used the term *dhimma* to refer to Jews. Hence, the religious restrictions that were imposed on Jews in the past continued to the beginning of the 20th century. During the 19th century it was still necessary for a Jewish man to wear a black *Jalaba* to distinguish them from Muslims who wore white one. Concerning Jewish women, they did not have any specific clothing. They dressed the traditional clothes similar to Muslims women and covered their hair.[194] Based on these attitudes of Moroccan sultans, the improvement of legal status of Jews in Morocco was not a priority on the political agenda of the Moroccan state. Thus, if there had been a significant improvement in the legal status of Jews in some al-

---

[193] Germain Ayache, "Jewish minority in pre-Colonial Morocco", *Revue Dar al-Niaba : études d'histoire marocaine*, 12, 1986: 7, quoted from Sharon Vance, The Martyrdom of a Moroccan Jewish Saint, 43.

[194] Joseph Tobi; Y Barnay; Shalom Bar-Asher; Samuel Ettinger; Michel Abitbol, *al-Yahūd fī al-Buldān al-Islāmīyah* [the Jews in Muslim Countries], 1850-1950 (al-Kuwayt : al-Majlis al-Waṭanī lil-Thaqāfah wa-al-Funūn wa- al-Ādāb, 1995), 313.

Maghrib countries, such as Algeria after the French occupation of Algiers in 1830, in Morocco, it was often seen as a result of activities of foreign interventions. Some were the result of the reforms in the Ottoman Empire in favor of its non-Muslim people. The others were the result of the influence of European powers, especially France, Spain, and Great Britain directly on Moroccan internal affairs and European Jewish organizations that intervened in favor of Moroccan Jews. The following is an attempt to understand the factors that led to the legal emancipation in the Jews' status in Morocco during the second half of the 19th century.

The Factors that Contributed to the Legal Emancipation in Jews' Status

There were many direct and indirect factors that contributed to the improvement of the legal status of Jews in Morocco during the second half of the nineteenth century. The prime contributing factor goes back to the reforms that conducted in Islamic countries (*al-Mashreq al-Islami*) that were under the rule of the Ottoman Empire in favor of the legal status of non-Muslims. The second factor was due to the direct interventions of foreign countries in Morocco and their military, commercial and political pressures on Morocco. The influences of European powers in Morocco were the direct factor that contributed to rethink in the legal status of Jews in Morocco.

The Indirect Factors (External factors).

The second half of the nineteenth century was known as the Legal Emancipation Era regarding the legal status of non-Muslims in the Islamic East. During this period, radical shifts occurred in the legal status of non-Muslims in the East with the growing of the intervention of European powers. In the wake of the French Revolution, both France and Great Britain made sure to grant the equal rights to their nationals of Jews and also to the Jews of the colonial Islamic East empires. In this sense, the Ottoman Empire also has seen a widespread movement of political, social and legal reforms. One of the manifestations of these reforms was that the authorities of the Ottoman Empire granted the equal rights to non-Muslim minorities.[195]

The Jews of the Ottoman Empire.

The legal status of Jews in Ottoman Empire was stable and had not seen any changes throughout the decades of the 16th century until the 18th century. However, the beginning of the nineteenth century was a turning point in the history of relationship between the Ottoman state and non-Muslim.[196]There were many external and internal factors which contributed to the change/reform in the Ottoman's attitude towards the legal status of Jews. These reforms were known in the Ottoman history as the *tanzimat*. Among the external factors that lead to such reforms, the growing of the interference of European powers in internal affairs of the Ottoman state, "through the reform provisions of the treaties of Paris (1856) and Berlin (1878), through the capitulations, which gave their subjects legal and fiscal privileges within the Ottoman Empire, and through the religious protectorates that particularly European powers asserted over particular groups of Ottoman Christians."[197] In another respect, the Ottoman Empire acquired the support of European powers against Russia during the war

[195] Ibid.,46.
[196] Ibid., 191.
[197] Stanford J. Shaw, Gökhan Çetinsaya, Ottoman Empire, *The Oxford Encyclopedia of the Islamic World*, http://www.oxfordislamicstudies.com/article/opr/t236/e0611# (accessed 12/12/2015).

(the Crimean War) of 1853-1856.[198] All these legal and fiscal privileges were related to the legal status of Jews and Christians of European communities living in Ottoman Empire and also to the indigenous Jews of the Ottoman Empire.[199] These reforms carried out through many phases known as *Tanzimat* period. It "planned under Sultan Mahmud (1808-1839), and were carried out under his sons Abdülmecid (Abd al-Majid) (1839–1861) and Abdülaziz ('Abd al-'Aziz) (1861–1876), and were brought to successful culmination under Sultan Abdülhamid II ('Abd al-Hamid) (1876–1909)."[200] The Sultan Mahmud II "did decide upon a number of measures of reform."[201] He granted Christians and Jews the right to equality with Muslims.[202] At his rise to rule in 1839, the Sultan 'Abd al-Hamid I, and late in summer 1839, issued a decree called *Hatt-ı Şerif Gülhane* (Imperial Rescript of Gülhane).[203] This decree was regarded as the first major reform in which "the state acknowledged basic rights to its citizens, Muslims and non-Muslims alike."[204] The edict lists many rights and duties of citizens and at the end it was stated that "these rights should be extend to all subjects, Muslims as well as non-Muslims."[205] It was also stated in decree (*farmân*) that "it is not possible to allow the persecution and torture of the Jewish people; therefore, they will enjoy under *Hatt-ı Şerif* all of the rights that granted to

---

[198] Joseph Tobi; Samuel Ettinger El la, *al-Yahūd fī al-Buldān al-Islāmīyah, 1850-1950*, 197.
[199] Hassān al-Zayn, *al-Awdā' al-Qānuniyya*, 26.
[200] Stanford J. Shaw, Gökhan Çetinsaya, "Ottoman Empire", http://www.oxfordislamicstudies.com/article/opr/t236/e0611# (Accessed 16/12/2015).
[201] Butrus Abu-Manneh, "the Islamic Roots of the Gülhane Rescript, Die Welt des Islams", New Series, Vol. 34, Issue 2 (Nov., 1994), pp. 181.
[202] Joseph Tobi; Samuel Ettinger El la, *al-Yahūd fī al-Buldān al-Islāmīyah, 1850-1950*, 46.
[203] Butrus Abu-Manneh, The Islamic Roots of the Gülhane Rescript, 191.
[204] Stanford J. Shaw, Gökhan Çetinsaya, "Ottoman Empire" , http://www.oxfordislamicstudies.com/article/opr/t236/e0611# (accessed 16/8/2015).
[205] Butrus Abu-Manneh, " the Islamic Roots of the Gülhane Rescript", 193.

people under our control."[206] The policy of reforms continued and, in 1856, released the constitutional reforms which were known as *Islâhat Hatt-ı Hümâyûnu* (Sultan's decree or the Imperial Rescript of Reforms of 1856) at the end of the Crimean War, in which the European powers stood beside Turkey against Russia.[207] According to the preamble of this decree, "this decree promised the security of citizens and their property and the preservation of their honour to all the subjects of my Empire without distinction of classes or of religion."[208] This decree addressed in details the rights of religious minorities such as the political rights. Based on this decree, *jiziyah* was abolished that was one of the manifestations of the distinction between Muslims and non-Muslims.[209] The reforms peaked in which "the state gave its [all] citizens political rights, turning the empire into a constitutional monarchy, with a constitution and a parliament in 1876."[210] Hence, by the 1876 constitution, the non-Muslim minorities were granted anything similar to other populations.

Algerian Jews.

The French occupation of Algeria in 1830 was welcomed by about 17,000 Jews "who had been oppressed by Turkish rules."[211] According to Samuel Ettinger, Algerian Jews declared the date of French occupation as their national holiday. They considered this occupation would bring them

---

[206] Joseph Tobi; Samuel Ettinger El la, *al-Yahūd fī al-Buldān al-Islāmīyah, 1850-1950*, 197.
[207] Ibid.
[208] *Rescript of Reform – Islahat Fermanı* (18 February 1856), (The translator is unknown), http://www.anayasa.gen.tr/reform.htm (Accessed 16/12/2015).
[209] Joseph Tobi; Samuel Ettinger El la, *al-Yahūd fī al-Buldān al-Islāmīyah, 1850-1950*, 198.
[210] Butrus Abu-Manneh, The Islamic Roots of the Gülhane Rescript, http://www.oxfordislamicstudies.com/article/opr/t236/e0611# (accessed 16/12/2015).
[211] Joseph Tobi; Samuel Ettinger El la, *al-Yahūd fī al-Buldān al-Islāmīyah*, 348.

liberation from oppression and also would grant to them anything. [212] France conducted many reforms regarding the legal status of Jews. The first thing that French authority did is that, in 1830, it issued an order to appoint one the sons of Bakri Jewish family in the position of the head of Jewish nation.[213] In 1841, the French authority issued a decree that abolished of all rabbinic courts and the application of the French Civil Code for Jews.[214] Although the French authority promised that Algerian Jews will enjoy the same rights of their friends in France, the Jews, though regarded as French nationals did not receive the right of French citizenship until 1870 under the Cremieux Decrees that granted the French citizenship to all Algerian Jews. Previously, there were many debates about granting Algerian Jews French citizenship before this decree. Among the enthusiasts for the granting of French citizenship to Algerian Jews was Isaac Moïse Crémieux. He was born in France in 1796 and became a lawyer. He was a defender of the freedom of the Jews. Thus, when he appointed to position as "a justice minister he passed the Crémieux Decrees on October 24th, 1870, which conferred citizenship onto the Jewish community, then totaling around 37,000."[215] Legally, this meant that Jews became French and had the right to vote and to participate in the French politics.

In fact, these radical shifts that occurred in the legal status of Jews in the Islamic East and also in the Morocco's neighbor, Algeria, had significant impact on the Jews of Morocco. These changes made Moroccan Jews look to European powers, as liberators from oppression. The Moroccan Jews began

---

[212] Ibid., 349.
[213] Ibid.,349.
[214] Ibid.,350.
[215] Evans, Martin, "Algeria's Jewish Question", *History Today*, Juley 2012, Vol. 62 Issue 7, 11.

to ask the Moroccan government to "implement *Tanzimat* like reforms instituted by the Ottoman sultan that would eliminate the legal disabilities associated by *dhimmi* status."[216] Regarding the impact of Crémieux Decree on Moroccan Jews, many Moroccans began to move to Algeria. After they obtained French citizenship they returned to Morocco with rights. So, they began to challenge the *dhimma* law by "coming to live in Morocco as foreigners."[217]

The Direct factors (Internal Factors).

Foreign powers and their direct interventions in Moroccan affairs played a significant role in the legal changing that occurred in the status of Jews in Morocco. The following is an attempt to understand special ways that were used by foreign powers to make this change happens during the mid-19th century.

The Growing Penetration of the European Powers in Morocco.

Moroccan history has shown that foreign powers in Morocco go back to pre-nineteenth century. In the eighteenth century, especially during the second half, one may argue that Sidi Muhammad b. 'Abd Allah (1757-1790) gave new breath to the international relationship through what the so-called "opening-up policy".[218] He concluded "numerous commercial treaties with the foreign powers"[219] because he "saw the advantage of foreign trade

---

216 Daniel J. Schroeter, "From Dhimmis to Colonized Subjects", 111.

217 Ibid.,110.

218 Amine Cohen, "Tujjar al-Sultan: Nukhab Yhudiyya fi Maghrib of the nineteenth century", *Nukhab Maghāribīyah: al-Marji'īyāt, al-Masārāt wa al-Adwār*, edited by Ibn 'Abdallāwī, al-Mukhtār, 2012, 83.

219 Daniel J. Schroeter, *the Sultan's Jew*, 13.

as a mean of securing revenue."[220] To succeed in his mission, he depended on rich Jewish families from different Moroccan cities. He agreed with them that each family send one of its members to the new city of Essaouira, especially with the establishment of the royal port in 1764.[221] Through this policy he was able to establish relationships between Jewish merchants and Christians.[222] The successive Sultans followed the same path of the Sultan Sidi Muhammad, especially when they saw the need for their country's close commercial relationship with Europe. However, as an exception, in the beginning of the nineteenth century, Mawlay Sulayman (1792-1822) had a different policy towards the relationship between Morocco and Europe.[223] Through this policy, which was marked as "closing policy", "Morocco appeared to be closing its doors to Europe in the age of European commercial expansion."[224] Among his policies, he prevented Moroccans from exporting the agriculture products to Europe.[225] At the same time, although the foreign trade was reduced in his reign; the Jews maintained their position in the royal court, in which, he continued to rely on Jews in diplomacy and "trade with European powers in Essaouira and Rabat in order to raise revenues to purchase weapons."[226] Following the death of Mawaly Sulayman, when Morocco wanted to reopen its doors again to Europe in the reign of Mawaly 'Abd al-Rahman (1822-1859), Algeria was

[220] Daniel J. Schroeter, "Royal Power and the Economy in Precolonial Morocco: Jews and the Legitimation of Foreign Trade", *In the Shadow of the Sultan*, edited by Rahma Bourqia and Susan Gilson Miller (Harvard University Press: 1999),79.
[221] Amine Cohen, *Tujjar al-Sultan*, 83.
[222] Daniel J. Schroeter, "Royal Power and the Economy in Precolonial Morocco", 79.
[223] Samuel Ettinger El la, *al-Yahūd fī al-Buldān al-Islāmīyah*, 281.
[224] Daniel J. Schroeter, *the Sultan's Jew*, 13.
[225] Amine Cohen, *Tujjar al-Sultan*, 80.
[226] Daniel J. Schroeter, "Royal Power and the Economy in Precolonial Morocco", 84.

occupied by the French in 1830.[227] This event was marked as additional pressure. Morocco became under the pressure for supporting the Algerian resistance based on the notion of *ummah*. On the other hand, the defeat of Moroccan Army by the French Army in Isly in 1844 showed the weakness of Morocco.[228] This marked a turning point in the relationship between Morocco and foreign powers in general. After this event, Morocco was forced to conclude with France two treaties; one in 1844 and the second in 1845. These two treaties with France opened the doors to other foreign countries to obtain more capitulations and commercial privileges. In this sense, under considerable pressure, Morocco concluded with the Great Britain a trade treaty, in 1856. This treaty opened the doors of Morocco for foreign businessmen because they, before the treaty, were confined to the port of Tangier.[229] When Spanish state saw these privileges that were obtained by the Great Britain, they began to ask Mawaly 'Abd al-Rahmān for the same privileges that were acquired by France and Great Britain.[230] In his work on the history of Morocco, Muhammad b. 'Abud points out that the Sultan 'Abd al-Rahmān was not afraid of the Spanish because of his friendship with Great Britain. Thus, he did not respond to the requests of Spain.[231] In 1859, the Spanish took advantage of a minor incident that occurred between Moroccans and Spanish in the border of Ceuta (Sibtah). Spanish declared war against Morocco in 1860. When Morocco lost this war, it concluded a peace treaty with Spain in 1860 and in 1861 a commercial

[227] Amine Cohen, *Tujjar al-Sultan*, 80.
[228] Daniel J. Schroeter, "From Dhimmis to Colonized Subjects", 110.
[229] Amine Cohen, *Tujjar al-Sultan*, 80.
[230] Muhammad b. 'Abud, *the History of Morocco* (Tetouan: 1951), 83.
[231] Ibid.

treaty.[232] These treaties were another military pressure after France challenged Moroccan sovereignty during the second half of the nineteenth century. Through these military, fiscal, commercial and political pressures, foreign countries were able to intervene in the internal affairs of Morocco.

The Policy of Foreign Powers towards Moroccan Jewry.

The intervention of foreign powers in Morocco was reflected in reality by several means.

The Texts (the Treaties).

When the European powers concluded treaties with Morocco, they did not forget to refer to non-Muslims in them, especially *jiziyah*. For instance, the treaty of 1856 with Great Britain stated in the article 3 that "the representative of the Queen of Great Britain in Morocco shall be at liberty to choose his interpreters and servants, either from Muslims or Jews, and neither his interpreters nor servants shall be compelled to pay any taxes or other similar, either a tax for Muslims or *jiziyah* for Jews." [233] Under this article, Morocco allowed Great Britain to intervene officially and legally in the affairs of its nationals. If this treaty did not give any other details concerning the rights of Jews, the Spain's treaties were clearer about this. Under the article 10 of the 1860 treaty, Morocco was forced to establish two churches in Morocco; one in Fes and second in Tetouan. In addition, Morocco was forced to respect and provide a special protection to the houses, churches, hospitals, and charitable institutions of non-Muslims. Based on this treaty, Morocco was forced to exempt non-Muslims from

[232] Abd al-Wahab b. Mansur, *the Problem of the Consulate Protection: From its Establishment into the Madrid Conference in 1888* (Rabat: 1985), 16-17.

[233] Ibid.,146.

paying taxes under any name.[234] Obviously, these treaties were the first challenges the *dhimma* law in Morocco by the foreign powers in which Jews found an opportunity to escape from the restrictions of Islamic law. These treaties, especially the treaty with Great Britain in 1856, used as method to emerge what the so-called consulate protection that most of Jews in Morocco preferred to be in. Thus, they caused the emergence of "a new privileged class of Jews, as protégés of European countries, escaped the jurisdiction of the *Makhzen*."[235]

The Protégé System and its Impact on the Legal Status of Jews.

The system of granting foreign protection (in Morocco known as a consular protection) to native Moroccan nationals is regarded as one of the most problems that challenged Moroccan government during the nineteenth century, especially in the second half.[236] At first, it was specified only for foreign consuls and their assistances such as vice-consuls, agents and also for European citizens who settled in Morocco for commercial and diplomatic proposes.[237] Muhammad Tahtah points out that the status of European citizens at the beginning was subjected to the provisions of Islamic teachings.[238] As the European powers obtained a large number of capitulations for their citizens in the Ottoman Empire, especially during the 19th century, they asked Morocco for more freedom to their citizens similar to the system of capitulations in the Ottoman Empire that allowed

234 Ibid.,16.

235 Daniel J. Schroeter, "From Dhimmis to Colonized Subjects", 112.

236 Turki Ajlan Al-Harithi, "the Changing status of Jews in Morocco", 197.

237 Muhammad Tahtah, "Brothers Enemies", 16 /01/2012. http://www.hespress.com/orbites/45471.html (Accessed 18/12/2015).

238 Ibid.

foreigners to enjoy "extraterritorial rights under the protection of their consulates."[239] Since Morocco believed such a system could be used to facilitate the trade with European countries, it "concluded similar treaties with foreign countries that granted foreign residents extraterritorial rights under the protection of their consulates."[240] Yet with the growth of European interests in Morocco during the nineteenth century, this system became a major "threat to Moroccan sovereignty" in which "the foreign consulates were issuing patents of protection to native agents who would also enjoy the protection of the foreign protection."[241] In the meantime, the system of foreign protection turned from its essential aim as a system of providing a protection to foreign citizens to a system that protected native Moroccans. This new status was seen by the Moroccan authority as a direct threat to its sovereignty, especially when the very people who received this protection were native Jews who were regarded as *dhimmis* that "the Islamic state was required to protect."[242] The history of Morocco has shown that native Jews were one of the Moroccan populations who benefited more from this system due to their knowledge of European languages and their relationships to European Jews.[243] The foreign consuls, who used the Jewish question as a means of achieving their commercial interests, appointed many Moroccan Jews to serve them as vice-consuls, interpreters, and agents.[244] The business competition between foreign countries, especially after the treaty with Great Britain in 1856, also had a directly influence on a

[239] Daniel J. Schroeter, "From Dhimmis to Colonized Subjet", 111.
[240] Daniel J. Schroeter, *the Sultan's Jew: Morocco and Sephardi World* (Stanford University Press: 2002), 125.
[241] Ibid.
[242] Ibid.
[243] Turki Ajlan Al-Harithi, "the Changing status of Jews in Morocco", 197.
[244] Daniel J. Schroeter, *the Sultan's Jew*, 121.

growing of number of Jewish protégé, in which Moroccan government became unable to control its nationals.[245] Daniel J. Schroeter in his study on Moroccan Jews and the Sharifian and French colonial state, indicates that "by the latter half of the 19th century, nearly every Moroccan Jewish merchant with any significant business with Europe became a protégé of a foreign state."[246] The American consul confirmed this fact. He mentioned that all the vice-consuls of the European countries were Jews except the vice-consuls of the Great Britain.[247] For instance, in 1858, the Spanish Consul, Juan Blanco, offered the foreign protection to almost 853 Jews in Morocco.[248] The consul of the United State, Felix Mathews, who was a Jew, also offered the American protection to the people of a whole village in Tangier which most of them were Jews. His successor, William Lewis, in 1887, described this village as an American colony in Morocco.[249] The phenomenon of offering protection to native Jews "become widespread and much abused."[250] The Jews who worked in the foreign consulates, in turn, played a big role in spreading the protections. Based on the idea of rescuing Jews from the deteriorating situations, they issued the certificate protection to their family members under the eyes of foreign consulates. For instance, in the town of Safi, (a city in western Morocco on the Atlantic Ocean) the representative of Spanish consul offered illegal certificate protections, where he offered too many to people who were under the protection of other countries.[251] Such behavior forced the governor of city to complain of

245 Turki Ajlan Al-Harithi, "the Changing status of Jews in Morocco", 197.
246 Daniel J. Schroeter, "From Dhimmis to colonized subjects", 111.
247 Turki Ajlan Al-Harithi, "the Changing status of Jews in Morocco", 193.
248 Ibid.,197.
249 Ibid.
250 Daniel J. Schroeter, *the Sultan's Jew*, 126.
251 Turki Ajlan Al-Harithi, "the Changing status of Jews in Morocco", 198.

this to the representative of Sultan in Tangier, Muhammad Bargach, asking him to stop such these illegal behaviors. Among what it was written in this letter "the Spanish consul offered too many illegal protections in the city and the tribes."[252] In the same direction went the vice-consul of Belgium in Casablanca, where he offered a large number of illegal protections to the Moroccans, especially Jews.[253]

Furthermore, the foreign protection has seen a remarkable development when the foreign consuls and the citizens of the foreign countries began to offer the certificate protection in exchange for amount money. Thus, it was sold to Moroccans, particularly Jews who hurried to buy it to change their legal status from *dhimmis* to one that ensured them new privileges. The sale of certificates of protections for some merchants became a source for their income. Hence, the foreign protection became easy to obtain; in addition to its price became subject to market forces.[254]

The Abuses of Jewish Protégé.

With the growing numbers of Jews who obtained the foreign protections, they enjoyed the capitulations similar to foreigners in Morocco, which were ensured by the treaties made with the European countries.[255] This led to "the Jews [who had obtained the foreign protection] were presented with new possibilities to cross interreligious boundaries."[256] Concerning the religious abuses, on the grounds that the protégé of foreign

---

252 Ibid.
253 Ibid.
254 Ibid.,198.
255 Ibid.,199.
256 Daniel J. Schroeter, "From Dhimmis to Colonized Subjects", 110.

countries enjoyed the rights in accordance with the treaties made with both Morocco and European countries, Jews began refusing to pay *jiziyah*. The treaties excluded the employees in the foreign consulates from paying *jiziyah* and other taxes.[257] Schroeter writes regarding the evasion by protégés; he points out that "one effect of the growth in the number of Jewish protégés was that many were not paying duties owed in the ports, especially in Tangier."[258] As instance of these duties, Schroeter refers to the evasion of payment of the *jiziyah* by protégés as symbolic importance in the legal status of Jews. He also indicates to what extent the non-payment of *jiziyah* was an important in the eyes of European powers. He indicates that in one report of the French consular agent in Essouira, August Beaumier, it was reported that "today this tax is reduced practically to nothing, as a consequence of the consular protection that the principal Jews have been able to obtain, to the extreme misery of the others."[259] The actions of Moroccan sultans towards those protégés were sometimes very harsh. For instance, in the *mallah* of Marrakesh during the period of the Sultan Sidi Muhammad, Jewish protégés began refusing to pay their *jiziyah*. The Sultan "ordered that those Jews who refused to pay should be expelled from the country and that a *talib* should be appointed to help carry this out."[260] Similar to that, in a letter from Mawlay al-Hassan to his representative in Fes, told him that he ordered the Jewish representative in Fez to collect *jiziyah* in accordance with the Islamic law, but he responded that Jews asked three months as a period to do so. Mawlay al-Hasan continued in his letter

---

[257] Turki Ajlan Al-Harithi, "the Changing status of Jews in Morocco", 200.
[258] Daniel J. Schroeter, "Royal Power and the Economy", 92.
[259] Ibid.
[260] Ibid.,93.

that their object was to allow the protégés enough time to write their protectors in the attempt to ask Moroccan government not to take it in accordance with the Islamic law.[261] In addition, they also refused to pay gate taxes (the *mukus*) that were important sources to Moroccan Treasury. Such these practices put the *Makhzen* in a difficult situation because it was unable to force the protégés to pay taxes or to adhere to Moroccan law.[262] Religious abuses were also shown by Moroccan Jews against Islam and Muslims in this period. A Jew dared to insult Islam in public places, and, in front of a Muslim judge in Safi. The Jew Isaac 'Ammar of Marrakesh, who insulted Islam, was refused by a notary to be appointed by a Muslim as a deputy of his business. As a result of this insult by the Jew, the governor of Safi wrote to the sultan regarding this religious abuse. The sultan ordered his representative in Tangier to write to the American consul in order stop such acts by Jews according to American laws, so that Muslims in Safi could be calmed.[263]

The International Political Support.

The existence of foreign consulates played a major role in making the world hear the voice of Moroccan Jews. Generally, the international political support reflected on the consulates reports, the published articles in the international and Zionist press and also by international Jewish sympathy through the western Jewish organizations.[264] The foreign consuls in Morocco had specific ways to justify using Jews as their representative in

[261] Turki Ajlan Al-Harithi, "the Changing status of Jews in Morocco", 200.
[262] Ibid.
[263] Ibid.,204.
[264] Amine Cohen, *Tujjar al-Sultan*, 90.

Morocco. In their reports to their countries regarding the life of Jews in Morocco, the consuls depicted that Jews were living in misery. They reported that Jews are governed by the *Dhimma* law that intervened in their personal affairs such as clothes and behavior, so they lost their rights.[265] This gloomy picture about the life of Jews brought the Jewish question great sympathy from the foreign governments. In a one letter that the American consul, Jesse Mcmath in Tangier had received, his government commanded him to use all possibilities to help the Moroccan Jews in the name of humanity.[266] Thus, the American consul helped the Jews as other foreign consuls did under pretext of helping Jews to save them from injustice and inequality.[267]

In addition to the reports of the consuls to their governments and the published articles in international Western and Zionist press, the Jewish organizations in Morocco also played a significant role in this context through the European and American Jewish Organizations. In the beginning 1860s of the nineteenth century, they began writing to the Jewish organizations in the west to intervene in favor of Moroccan Jews. In 1883, the Jews of Tangier sent a letter to the Jewish organizations of London, and New York. In this letter, they described the bad status of Jews. They also critiqued the Moroccan government about the death penalty that has been implemented on some Moroccan Jews. They asked foreign governments to

265 Turki Ajlan Al-Harithi, "the Changing status of Jews in Morocco", 193.
266 Ibid.
267 Ibid.

put Jews under their protection. This letter was also sent to the representatives of foreign countries in Tangier by Musa B. Brent.[268]

Among the international pressures on Morocco the visit of the leader of London's Jewish community, Sir Moses Montefiore to Morocco. He asked his government to allow him to visit Morocco, and to help him for arranging a meeting with the Sultan, "on a mission to obtain equal rights for Moroccan Jews."[269] Thus, The U.K. consul, John Hay, arranged this meeting and wrote to the Great Vizier of the Sultan in Marrakech to tell him about the visit of Sir Montefiore to the Sultan. Montefiore arrived to Marrakech in 1864. After days, the meeting was hold between Sultan and Montefiore, and they discussed the situations of Jews in Morocco. After two meetings with Sultan Muhammad, he was able to convince the Sultan to free two Jews from jail because they were accused of killing a Spanish man.[270] In the end, Montefiore "succeeded in obtaining a decree that promised the Jews justice and an end to corporal punishment."[271] In fact, the aim of Montefiore in his visiting was to convince Moroccan Sultan to carry out reforms in the legal status of Jews, as their nationals, similar to the *Tanzimat* reforms in the Ottoman Empire. According to Khalid b. al-Sghir, Montefiore promised the Sultan, by doing so; he will receive the support of the European countries similar to what they did with Ottoman Empire.[272] In his comment about this decree and comparing with the reforms of Ottoman Empire, Schroeter states that

[268] Ibid.

[269] Daniel J. Schroeter, *the Sultan's Jew*, 153.

[270] Turki Ajlan Al-Harithi, "the Changing status of Jews in Morocco",

[271] Daniel J. Schroeter, *the Sultan's Jew*, 153.

[272] Khalid b. al-Sghir, *Morocco and Great Britain in the Nineteenth Century 1856-1886* (Casablanca: al-Najah al-Jadida, 1997), 299.

whereas the Tanzimat reforms in the Ottoman Empire effectively did away with *dhimmis* status, and established new civil courts, the Moroccan sultan was from his point of view simply ratifying the existing system of justice within the framework of Islamic law: in other words, no civil status with equality for all was established, and Jews continued to pay *jiziyah*.[273]

Increasingly, over the years of the second half of the 19th century, the international political support, particularly by Jewish Organizations and the United State, continued through diplomatic missions and the western consuls in Morocco. For instance, in the beginning of 1870s, the Jewish organizations in Paris asked the French Ministry of Foreign Affairs to ask the Moroccan Sultan to remove injustice and oppression on Jews.[274] In 1873, under the pressures of Jewish organizations, the U.K. consul, John Hay, in Tangier, submitted a protest to the Sultan demanding a good treatment for the Jews of Rabat and Meknes.[275]

Additionally, the other factor that also contributed to the deterioration of the legal status of Jews in Morocco is the growing influence of the European-style education that offered by the universal Jewish organizations such as the Alliance Israélite Universelle. After two years of its establishment in Paris in 1860, the organization opened its first school in Morocco, in1862, in the city of Tetouan.[276] Through this school Jews introduced to modern education on the European-style. Thus, they

---

273 Daniel J. Schroeter, *the Sultan's Jew*, 153.
274 Turki Ajlan Al-Harithi, "the Changing status of Jews in Morocco",
275 Ibid.
276 Amine Cohen, *Tujjar al-Sultan*, 89-90.

connected directly with the European civilization, and also they learned modern Western concepts concerning modern society.[277] Consequently, their integration with the European began to increase. This process continued during the French and Spanish protectorate periods.

Therefore, despite the fact that these ways that offered by the foreign countries, particularly European powers, helped Moroccan Jews to escape *dhimmi* status, they were not legal changes enacted by the Sultan. Thus, after the Jews were looking for European intervention as a way to obtain a new status that could rescue them from the Islamic rule, it turned to a way that contributed to the deterioration of their legal status, and they lived in a difficult situation more than even before. Instead, they became subjects or protégé of European countries. Therefore, after the Jews were used by Moroccan Sultans to limit the influence of Europe in Morocco, now, they became ways of the European penetration.

Conclusion

The aim of this chapter was to examine the factors that contributed to the changes that took place in the legal status of Jews during the second half of the nineteenth century. This chapter argues that the growing penetration of the European powers in Morocco had an essential contribution to the transformation of Jews from the nationals of that Sultan to a problem. This manifested in two things; the first one is the issue of foreign protection, which was an essential issue that indicated the inability of Sultan to control his nationals; the second thing manifested in the international political

[277] Muhammad Tahtah, "Brothers Enemies", 16 /01/2012. http://www.hespress.com/orbites/45471.html (Accessed 20/12/2015).

support in which Jews took advantage of their relations with the Europeans. They began to receive the international sympathy with their issue. These two things contributed to the legal and political emancipation of Jews from the Islamic state, represented by the Sultan. On the other hand, this chapter argues the legal status of Jews in this period had seen considerable deterioration because, instead, they obtained new reforms in their status; they became subjects or protégé of the European countries.

CHPTER III

-

The Legal Jews' Status under the French Protectorate

As it has been seen in the previous chapter, the preliminary precursors of the improvement in the legal Moroccan Jews' status began in the mid-19th century as a result of the external and internal factors. The Moroccan Jews benefited more from the foreign influences, especially the European intervention. Considering that, in the latter half of the 19th century, the legal status of Jews in other Muslim countries had changed as in Algeria and Tunisia, the Moroccan Jews, in their turn, began to look for obtaining the same privileged status. Moroccan Jews regarded the European powers, especially France, as the saviors that would rescue them from a distressing situation. In this respect, Moroccan Jews welcomed the arrival of the foreign protectorate, especially the arrival of France in 1912.[278] This chapter will shed light on the evolving legal status of the Jewish community of Morocco during the protectorate period, especially who were under the French colonial authorities. It will focus on two related aspects of Moroccan Jewish legal life: the protectorate policy toward Jews about the legal status and the kind of identity that Jews finally obtained, especially in the midst of conflict between often-conflicting interest groups: the Moroccan nationalism and Zionism about who will assimilate/mobilize more Jews. It will focus mainly on the Jews who were under the French protectorate because they suffered a lot more than those who were under Spanish protectorate or who were in Tangier, especially during the Vichy Government.

[278] Daniel J. Schroeter, "From Dhimmis to Colonized Subjects", 113.

The Foreign Protectorate Policy toward the Legal Jews' Status.

In the turn of the 20th century, the elite of Jewish communities were influenced by freedom, rights and other privileges that were granted to Jews living both in France and the French colonies in North Africa such as Algeria as well as by the Western modernity. Therefore, they were eager to join French modernity to be emancipated from religious restrictions and to modernize themselves. They "believed that the conquering Western powers would bring emancipation from the oppressive environment of Islamic despotism, rescuing the Jewish communities from the decay that surrounded them and setting them on the course of Western progress and enlightenment." [279] The eagerness of emancipation made Moroccan Jews viewed the foreign protectorate as a way of evolution. They very "welcomed the advent of the foreign protectorate as a vehicle to achieve emancipation (the end to dhimmi status and the beginning of a civil culture under enlightened International protectorate),"[280] especially the arrival of French protectorate to Morocco. In the dissociation that follows, it would be highlighted on what was made for Jews by the French authorities.

The French Protectorate Policy toward Jews.

The French protectorate policy towards Jews was very complicated and ambiguous. Scholars, such as Daniel J. Schroeter and Joseph Chetrit, often describe the policy of the French protectorate authorities towards Jews was to control them and use them in their interest rather than to change or

[279] Daniel J. Schroeter, ET. "Emancipation and Its Discontents", 173.
[280] Ibid,.171.

improve their legal status.[281] In this regard, Daniel J. Schroeter and Joseph Chetrit note:

> the legal changes in the Jews' status and the reforms communal institutions were designed by the colonial regime more to control the Jewish communities and their internal organization than fundamentally to transform the Jewish communities as the emancipatory rhetoric implied.[282]

The beginning of the 20th century witnessed the conflict between France, Britain, Spain, and Germany of commercial, strategic, diplomatic dominance in Morocco. This conflict led finally to the so-called "the Treaty of Green Island" (*Mu'ahdat al-Jazirah al-Khadra*) in 1906. It agreed/decided between the four parties and the Sultan Moulay Abdelaziz (1894-1908) to make Morocco an International protectorate.[283] In accordance with the 1906 treaty, Morocco was divided into three Zones. France got the Eastern and Southern parts, Spain got the Northern part, while Tangier was declared an International Zone.[284] Many clauses of this treaty were included in the treaty protection of Fez that was signed between France and Morocco on March, 1912.[285] The 1912 treaty states that the French colonial authorities undertake to respect the Islamic religion and to maintain religious institutions,[286] which means implicitly maintaining the legal status of *ahl al-Dhimma* as it was. The 1912 treaty also provides that it is necessary to keep

---

281 Daniel J. Schroeter, "From Dhimmis to Colonized Subjects", 116.
282 Daniel J. Schroeter, ET. "Emancipation and Its Discontents", 171.
283 Muhammad Tahtah, "Brothers Enemies",16 /01/2012.. http://www.hespress.com/orbites/45471.html (Accessed 02/03/2016).
284 Ibid.
285 Muhammad Kenbib, *Moroccan Jews, 1948-1912*, 34.
286 Ibid.

the sovereignty and integrity of the Moroccan state, especially what related to religious and political status enjoyed by the Sultan.[287] In practice, Morocco was ruled by the representative of France (the General Resident, the highest French official in Morocco), but, as symbol, the Sultan kept his right to "ratify" or not the decrees issued by the Resident General. Therefore, the policy of the Resident General Lyautey in Morocco was to retain the status of the Sultan "as the respected symbol of the state and to return the Makhzen to its former glory, while strictly limiting its authority"[288]as was before the protectorate. Lyautey "believed that Morocco, unlike Algeria, should not be annexed to France, nor should it be considered a "colony"; rather, it was to remain sovereign but "protected"..." [289] Therefore, once, Lyautey argues that "in Morocco, there is one government, the Sharifian government, protected by France." [290] He promised that, in Morocco, he would not defend tradition or change custom but rather to develop and civilize Moroccan society." [291] By this, "France opened Morocco to Western influence in 1912 without altering the foundation and structure of the Sultan's theocratic power."[292] Thus, under the protectorate, the Sultan continued to play a role in internal politics of the country, and therefore, Jews became living between two powers, colonial authorities, and, with necessary, their commitment to permanent allegiance to the Sultan.

---

[287] Susan Gilson Miller, *A History of Modern Morocco* (Cambridge University Press 2013), 90-91.

[288] Ibid.,91.

[289] Ibid.,90.

[290] Ibid.,91.

[291] Ibid.,90.

[292] Andre Chouraqui, *The Social and Legal Status of the Jews of French Morocco*, 7.

To avoid the same mistake that had been made in Algeria the granting Jews French citizenship, the Jewish policy of Lyautey in Morocco was to keep the status quo, where "Moroccan Jews were to remain subjects of the Sultan".[293] "Although there were advocates for granting Moroccan Jews French citizenship, especially among some of the westernized Jewish elites and their Franco-Jewish supports, the French authorities clearly had no intention of adopting the Algerian policy."[294] During the first days of French protectorate rule under Lyautey, theoretically, it was acknowledged the equality between Muslims and Jews, where they moved from the status as *dhimmis* to the status as "subjects" to the Sultan.[295] The purpose of this policy was to please *'Ulama* and mobilize their support and sympathy. It was also to "avoid agitating the Muslim population against French rule."[296] On the contrary, at the same time, Lyautey wanted to mobilize the sympathy of Jews to succeed in his mission in Morocco. Accordingly, in practical term, and in the absence of any legal text and without mentioning officially to change the legal Jews' status, it was decided to abolish *jiziyah* and other exceptional and arbitrary taxes. They eliminated all discriminatory practices related to the status of Jews as *dhimmis* such as housing, clothing in all Moroccan areas.[297] According to Andre Chouraqui,

> French authorities guaranteed to Jews the right to live where and as they please, the freedom of dress and movement, the right to own land outside the Mellah, exemption from special taxes

293

294 Daniel Schroeter, "the Origins and Identity of Indigenous North African Jews", 174.

295 Muhammad Tahtah, "Brothers Enemies",16 /01/2012. http://www.hespress.com/orbites/45471.html (Accessed 12/3/2016).

296 Daniel Schroeter, "the Origins and Identity of Indigenous North African Jews", 174

297 Robber Arsuf, *Moroccan Jews and Muhammad V*, 76.

imposed upon certain non-Moslems and protection from general persecution.[298]

As a practical example, in Fez, it was allowed for Jews to move out of the *Mellahs* into the new city and lived in Muslims neighborhood regarding they became of an equal footing with Muslims.[299] Through the legal elimination of the *dhimmi* status and *jiziyah*, in practice, Lyautey showed his good will to Jews and towards their legal status. In this respect, he was very keen to visit Jews in their neighborhood,[300] to show his keenness in improving their status.

However, although what was done to improve the legal Jews' status in Morocco and the goodwill shown by Lyautey towards Jews, they were not happy with his policy as long as there was no legal text framing clearly their status. So, the Jewish elite who wished to obtain French nationality *en masse* resisted the Lyautey's policy and strongly pressed through influential French Jewish organizations to change the legal status of Jews by "naturalizing them as French "citizens."[301] But, despite these pressures, all their attempts to achieve a new legal status did not lead to anything. Even Presidential decree on naturalization of foreigners in Morocco, issued on April 29, 1920 by the President of the French Republic, did not mention Moroccan Jews. They remained out of any legislative text/lawmaking.[302] For example, in 1913, the Alliance Israélite Universelle (AIU) provided a

---

298 Andre Chouraqui, *The social and Legal Status of the Jews of French Morocco*, 7
299 Robber Arsuf, *Moroccan Jews and Muhammad V*, 76.
300 Muhammad Kenbib, *Moroccan Jews, 1948-1912*, 36.
301 Jonathan Wyrtzen, M.A, "Constructing Morocco",223.
302 Muhammad Tahtah, Brothers Enemies, 16 /01/2012.
http://www.hespress.com/orbites/45471.html (accessed 12/3/2016).

request to French authorities to make Jews outside the Islamic legal system and put them under the French judiciary.[303] They issued this based on the fact that the Jews are considered as second /subjects "citizens" within the framework of Islamic law. However, there was no response from the French authorities, which made the AIU submit a second request seven years later in 1920.[304] In general, if it had put an end to discrimination associated with the status of Jews as *dhimmis*, their legal status did not see radical changes. After the Jews' disappointment to obtain the French nationality, they continued to live under an ambiguous status. As subjects of the Sultan, they were under the patronage of the Sultan. Since they were considered *dhimmis*, they had no right to appoint for power positions in the framework of the *Makhzen*, and they were prevented from being employed in the protectorate administration because they were Moroccan "citizens" or "subjects". During the protectorate period, there were no favorable conditions for Jews to achieve an identity outside the Islamic religious frame.

Reforms in the Framework of the French Policy.

After six years of the coming of the French protectorate, and under the pressures of the Jewish communities in Morocco and some International Jewish organizations, the Resident General, in 1918, began to apply reforms on the internal organization of the Jewish communities. On 22 May, 1918, it was issued two *zahirs* that re-regulate the Jewish communities and the Jewish courts system in the framework of the so-called "Freedom under the

303 Ibid.
304 Ibid.

control of the French authorities."[305] The first one provided for the establishment new "committees" of the Jewish communities in each city. Under this *zahir*, the presidency of these committees had to be from the dignitaries (*A'ayan*). Thus, it became the senate (the house of *A'ayan*) are appointed by (the Grand Vizier), the Prime Minister rather than the Jewish communities.[306] They possessed jurisdiction only over charity works, and the matters of worship. Concerning personal status it was under the jurisdiction of the religious Jewish courts.[307] Another new reform was the updating of judicial system. Concerning the second *zahir*, it "systematized a hierarchal structure for the Jewish court system in Morocco and brought it more directly under the control of the Ministry of Justice." [308] Based on this *zahir*, it was established:

> in Rabat, a high rabbinic court of appeals. The Moroccan rabbinical courts possessed jurisdiction only over "Moroccan Jews" (Jews of other nationalities were under the French court system in the Protectorate) and only ruled on personal status issues (including marriage, filiation, divorce, adoption, the validation of testimony, probate, and donations). Any other civil or criminal litigation was under the jurisdiction of the Sharifian court system, administered by qaids or pashas.[309]

---

305 Muhammad Tahtah, "Brothers Enemies", 16 /01/2012. http://www.hespress.com/orbites/45471.html (accessed 12/3/2016).

306 Robber Arsuf, *Moroccan Jews and Muhammad V*, 78.

307 Jonathan Wyrtzen, M.A, "Constructing Morocco", 226.

308 Ibid., 227.

309 Ibid.,226.

Consequently, based on these reforms, the old intuitions were replaced by the committees that did not have any elements of authority, and their jurisdiction confined only over margin of maters such as charity and religious affairs. In addition, the election of the president of committees and the approval of budget were administered by the pashas to be accepted. In judicial system, no longer did the Rabbis elect judges; instead, they were nominated by the Grand Vizier. The jurisdiction of judges was also limited only to the personal status. As Daniel Schroeter indicates "the Jews were granted a level of autonomy with the notion of preserving their native institutions, under the surveillance of the colonial state."[310] Another important reform in the judicial system was the establishment of a high rabbinic court of appeals. The first president of this court was the Grand Rabbi of Sale, Raphael Encaoua.[311] To put the Jewish communities more under the control of French authorities, in 23 June, 1919, the Resident General established a new post the so-called "the inspector of "Israeli Institutions." [312] The inspector was in charge of the internal control of the Jewish communities, and provided advice related to the special Jewish issues, both at the political and religious level.[313] "As an official liaison with the Residency, the President of the Casablanca Community Committee, Yahya Zagury (who was actually a naturalized French citizen) was initially appointed as the inspector of "Israelite institutions." [314] By appointing this man, the Residency was able to put the Jewish communities under its direct

[310] Daniel Schroeter, "the Origins and Identity of Indigenous North African Jews", 174.
[311] Robber Arsuf, *Moroccan Jews and Muhammad V*, 88.
[312] Ibid.
[313] Muhammad Tahtah, "Brothers Enemies", 16 /01/2012.
http://www.hespress.com/orbites/45471.html (accessed 17/3/2016).
[314] Jonathan Wyrtzen, M.A, "Constructing Morocco", 227.

control, because Yahya Zagury was considered by the French as one of their loyalist, especially for his role during the event of Casablanca in 1907.[315] Thus, it can be said these reforms and such appointments were designed to limit the autonomy of the Jewish communities rather than to improve the legal status of them. In general

> the shortcoming of the reforms, however, was that no structure was put in place to coordinate between the individual committees, a grievance that, in addition to the non-democratic appointment process for committee members, became a central demand for reform by the Jewish communities later in the 1940s.[316]

Additionally, in 1938, French authorities issued a new law that gave the Jews the right to equal access to the state posts. It canceled the old one, which prevented non-Muslims from the exercise of power on behalf of the Sultan. In 1945, there was another reform to re-regulate the structure of the Jewish community. In which it established an organization comprised of the various members of the Jewish communities that they were elected by the Jews.[317] The purpose of this organization was to represent the Moroccan Jewish communities at the French-Moroccan Government. Its meetings were held once a year in Rabat for consultations among its members under the supervision of the French authorities. Later, another reform came in 1947, the French authorities decided to allow the Jews to be members in the council of state.[318]

---

[315] Robber Assaraf, *Moroccan Jews and Muhammad V*, 89.
[316] Jonathan Wyrtzen, M.A, "Constructing Morocco", 227.
[317] Robber Assaraf, *Moroccan Jews and Muhammad V*, 88.
[318] Ibid.

Jews and the Moroccan National Movement.

At the beginning of the 1930s, the Moroccan National movement was established in an atmosphere full of tension caused by the so-called Berber *zahir* that was issued by the French protectorate on May 16, 1930. Its emergence came as a reaction against Barber "*zahir* that had created different legal systems for Moroccans, where it divided Moroccans to two ethnic groups Barber (*Imazighen*) and Arab."[319] This led to the rise of the controversy over the legal status of Jews, and their nationality, and identity again, but this time by the Moroccan Muslims. In reality, it seems that there was a new language of equality where began to rise in Moroccan Muslim spoken, especially by the Moroccan nationalists. In 1933, the nationalists began to declare that the Jews are Moroccan citizens and after gaining the independence for Morocco, they would enjoy the same rights and duties like all Moroccans.[320] The efforts that were made by the Moroccan National Movement to mobilize the Jewish support eventually led to open discussions between nationalists and Moroccan Jewish leaders about the future in the press. In this respect, a group of nationalists connected with the royal palace, requesting the Sultan Muhammad V cancel Berber *zahir*, affirming that, in Morocco, there are officially only two religions Islam and Judaism.[321] Moroccan National movement intensified its activities and met with the Sultan again in 1934. This time they connected with the royal palace directly and regularly in order to prepare the program of reforms the

[319] Muḥammad V, Encyclopedia Britannica, http://www.britannica.com/biography/Muhammad-V-sultan-of-Morocco#ref182890 Last Updated 8-4-2015 (accessed 20/3/2016).

[320] Muhammad Tahtah, "Brothers Enemies", 16 /01/2012. http://www.hespress.com/orbites/45471.html (accessed 20/3/2016).

[321] Robber Assaraf, *Moroccan Jews and Muhammad V*, 127.

so-called the demands of the Moroccan people in 1934 (The 1934 Plan de Réformes). It was agreed to submit this document on 1 December, 1934 to the French prime minister, the Resident General, and the Sultan.[322] This document discussed in details a series of demands for far-reaching reforms in various areas: political, economic, social and juridical. The demand that was relevant to discussion in this chapter is the demand about the democratization of life. In the Nationalists' view, and in order to create a democratic life in society, they requested to set up direct elections in which Moroccan Muslims and Jews would participate only.[323] They "proposed granting equal civic rights to all Moroccans (Muslim and Jewish) and called for universal suffrage without distinction to religion in the election of Moroccan representatives councils at the municipal and national level".[324] For the first time, an official document prepared by Muslims put Jews and Muslims on an equal footing without consideration of religious distinction. Thus, it can be said that the demands and suggestions of nationalists were very advanced. In this regard, the Nationalists continued their activity in order to achieve "national consensus", both Jews and Muslims, against the French protectorate. Muhammad Kenbib, in his article "the Sultan Muhammad V and the collective Memory of the Jews", shows that the Muslim nationalists spoke with the Jewish intellectuals in order to convince them not to ask for the French or Spanish nationality. They requested Jews to join together to fight to improve the living situation of the various

[322] Ibid,.131
[323] Ibid,.132
[324] Jonathan Wyrtzen, M.A, "Constructing Morocco", 245.

components of the "Moroccan people," Jews and Muslims[325] In addition, one of the nationalist, Muhammad al-Khloti wrote several articles in the newspaper (*L'Action du people*) addressing and reminding the Jews that they are Moroccan citizens and that Morocco is for all Moroccans, Jews and Muslims, inviting Jews to participate, with Muslims, effectively in the defense of the homeland against the foreign protectorate.[326] In one of his articles, in August 1932, he addressed a story that happened to him with his Jewish friends who asked about the attitude of youth Muslims towards Muslim-Jewish relations in the future. According to Jonathan Wyrtzen, in al-Kholti's response, he emphasized on

> the historic solidarity of Moroccan Muslims and Jews, contrasting the tolerance and freedom Jews have enjoyed since they took refuge in Morocco with the European Christian anti-Semitism displayed in the "pogroms of the Romanians" and the "Hitlerian inquisition in Germany." He also stressed the importance of solidarity between Moroccan Jews and Muslims with regard to the injustice of the French Protectorate system. Responding to a campaign by a Casablanca lawyer, Mr. Busquet, to renew demands that Morocco's Jews be naturalized as French citizens, Kholti argues this would violate the 1912 treaty and foment discord between the two races by inaugurating an era of favoritism for a minority in the country: "For the jurisdictions, it is necessary to

[325] Muhammad Kenbib, Sultan Sidi Mohammed Ben Youssef, http://www.minculture.gov.ma/index.php/2010-01-11-01-40-04/etudes-essaie/555-mohamed-kenbib-sultan-sidi-mohamed (accessed 21/3/2016).

[326] ibid.

> admit that the Muslim suffers like them, from the same evil. We cannot apply there, too, two weights and two measures."[327]

The next months and in the same newspaper (*L'Action du people*) as a response to al-Kholti's article, there were several articles written, but this time, by Moroccan Jews that confirmed the historic solidarity and Moroccan Muslim-Jewish unity. Wyrtzen, in his research, addresses that a Jewish leader from Fes, Isaac Bendayan in 1928 wanted to create an association "*Etihad el Shabiba Islamia Isra'ilia el Magribia*", but it was rejected by the French authorities.[328] He also shows that Al-Kholti in his articles addressed the legal status of Jews, where he affirmed that "Jews and Muslims should be treated an equal treatment and equal participation in the political domain:

> For I consider that he [the Jew] is Moroccan, and that he must be treated like other Moroccans without consideration of religious ideas that he professes, which remain for me an element of personal belief which does not affect the will of us who want to see our country unified under the reciprocal tolerance of a penetrating liberalism. The Jews born and living in Morocco are Moroccans. The international and political contingencies created by the "Metropole" cannot be decided otherwise, without annulling the contract with the Sultan.[329]

The discussion between the nationalists and Jewish notables and intellectuals about the definition of identity did not stop, but it continued over the next years of ambiguity in the legal Jewish status especially in

327 Jonathan Wyrtzen, M.A, "Constructing Morocco", 242.
328 Ibid.
329 Ibid,.243.

1937. Despite these repeated calls of the nationalists to Jewish intellectuals who wanted to integrate in French culture in order to build unity there was no response to these calls from Jews. They (Moroccan Jews) put their hopes in French protectorate to rescue them from the status quo. However, when the World War II broke out in France and its colonies, the Jewish hopes quickly faded. "Jews in Morocco quickly faced a transition to Vichy legislation, in 1941, which would destroy their confidence that the "Protector" could be trusted. This experience seriously challenged any remaining hope that cultural assimilation would yield political rights."[330]

Vichy and the Status of Jews: Jews Not Frenchman.

After the outbreak of World War II, the French state, under Marshal Petain following the Nazi regime, enacted racial laws against Jews and applied them on Moroccan Jews starting from 1941. These new laws forced the state to expel all Jews from the public offices and to impose more restrictions on them in all fields.[331] As the Resident General, in Rabat, was loyal to Vichy regime, the Jews experienced difficult conditions. According to Robber Assaraf, in the midst of this, the Jews appealed for help from the royal palace. They sent urgent requests to the Sultan to abandon or not to adopt the *zahir* legislation, which was issued by the Resident General based on the French law of June 3, 1941. The *Zahir* established the racist procedures against Moroccan Jews. In accordance with the Islamic law requirements, they emphasized that the Sultan Muhammad V would violate *al-Sharī'a* law if he ratified this *zahir* of these actions which are contrary to the Quranic text. They justified that the Sharia law allows *Ahl al-Dhimma*:

[330] Ibid,.
[331] Ibid,.251

Christians and Jews to live in *Dar al-Islam* and to exercise all crafts and trades as long as they pay *jiziyah* and respect the Islamic religion.[332] In this regard, Robber Assaraf states that the Sultan, under Jewish request, met with some Jewish nobles in his Royal palace in Rabat many times, in May, June and August 1942. The first meeting was in secret and in an isolated and dark room.[333] According to the president of the Jewish community of Meknes, the Jews were hidden in a covered truck when they entered to the royal palace. In these meetings, the Sultan Mohamed V expressed explicitly his sympathy to their status. In addition, he affirmed their right to enjoy the protection of the law, stressing the equal treatment that must be provided to them just like the Muslim subjects.[334] Concerning the *zahir* and the racial actions, the Sultan assured that he had not been able to cancel it, but he promised that he would do to mitigate its influence for not applying it literally.[335] The news about meetings and declarations of the Sultan Muhammad V about the Vichy laws quickly arrived to the French Jewish communities in France. In this respect, the coming reports from the intelligence of the Vichy government pointed out that there was a claim within the Jewish communities in the French free Zone showed that the Sultan rejected the application of French law against the Jews. The reports also point out that the Jews of France declared publicly that the Government of France should had asked the Sultan to give it lessons in tolerance.[336]

---

[332] Muhammad Kenbib, Sultan Sidi Mohammed Ben Youssef, http://www.minculture.gov.ma/index.php/2010-01-11-01-40-04/etudes-essaie/555-mohamed-kenbib-sultan-sidi-mohamed (accessed 21/3/2016).

[333] Robber Arsuf, *Moroccan Jews and Muhammad V*, 226.

[334] Muhammad Kenbib, Sultan Sidi Mohammed Ben Youssef, http://www.minculture.gov.ma/index.php/2010-01-11-01-40-04/etudes-essaie/555-mohamed-kenbib-sultan-sidi-mohamed (accessed 21/3/2016).

[335] Robber Assaraf, *Moroccan Jews and Muhammad V*, 226.

[336] Ibid.

Because of the resistant procedures toward Jews which were unpopular in addition to the attitudes of the Sultan, the Resident was forced to reduce the application of the Vichy law. For example, the Alliance schools continued to work normally. The Jewish teachers and professors, who were expelled from the French institutions, were allowed to apply for job and work in the Alliance schools. Concerning the legal procedures linking to the expulsion of Jews from European neighborhoods it applied only to the families who owned houses in these neighborhoods after September 1939. Concerning the procedures relating to the property declaration they were applied also only to the properties which were worth more than 5000 francs. It excluded the furniture and jewelry and personal items.[337] In this changing of French attitude toward the Jews shows clearly how "this turning of the tables created an incentive for the Moroccan Jews to take refuge in their dhimmi status in the French zone, allying with the *Makhzen* against the Resident"[338].

In the midst of the struggle of the Jews against the Vichy law, another event happened that had a significant impact on the legal status of Jews. The date of November 8th, 1942 was the dramatic change for Moroccan Jews. It was the date of arrival/landing of American troops on Moroccan coast in the framework of "the Anglo-American invasion of North Africa, "Operation Torch."[339] For Jews this event was considered the Divine salvation[340] from the anti-Jewish law, so that the "arrival of American troops in Morocco was ecstatically welcomed by Moroccan Jews."[341] As Robber Assaraf shows, the

[337] ibid.
[338] Jonathan Wyrtzen, M.A, "Constructing Morocco", 261.
[339] Ibid.,262.
[340] Robber Assaraf, *Moroccan Jews and Muhammad V*, 237.
[341] Jonathan Wyrtzen, M.A, "Constructing Morocco", 262.

enthusiasm of the Jews about the arrival of the Americans led them to believe that the time of French domination in Morocco is over. This "was an evident in a Judeo-Arabic song that circulated through the country's mellahs, "Get out O French, Morocco is not yours. America has come to take it, your domination is over!."[342] They also chanted Judeo-Arabic words glorifying the Sultan.[343] However, their hopes were given up because the arrival of America did not put "the immediate end to Vichy rule in North Africa, as the Allies chose to keep the French administration in place."[344] The implementation of the anti-Jews legislation continued on Jews both in Algeria and Morocco. Therefore, the legal status of Jews itself was not immediately improved either, but the American Jewish organizations played a major role as a lobby for pressures to end the Vichy Government's policy in North Africa.[345] They made significant pressures on Roosevelt[346] to revoke the Vichy law through the Jewish American press in the U.S. These pressures "led him to force the French Commander of North Africa, Henri Giraud, to break completely with Vichy, including a measure that abrogated all racial legislation in North Africa."[347] On 15 March, 1943, the French authorities issued a memorandum that put an end to the racial legislation to Jews in North Africa and Morocco.[348]

---

[342] Robber Arsuf, *Moroccan Jews and Muhammad V*, 238.

[343] Ibid.

[344] Jonathan Wyrtzen, M.A, "Constructing Morocco", 262.

[345] Ibid.

[346] (January 30, 1882 – April 12, 1945), he was an American statesman and political leader who served as the President of the United States from 1933 to 1945. https://en.wikipedia.org/wiki/Franklin_D._Roosevelt. (accessed 17/4/2016).

[347] Ibid.,263.

[348] Robber Arsuf, Moroccan Jews and Muhammad V, 241.

In the Moroccan side, on 23 January, 1943, the Sultan Muhammad V ordered the Grand Vizier Muhammad al-Maqri, to connect secretly with Americans, especially with Henry Morgenthau, Jr.[349]. The purpose was to know the U.S. attitude about the future of Morocco. It was also to remind the Americans about the traditional status of Jews as well as the measures that enabled them to escape from the Vichy racial laws.[350] In their contacts, al-Maqri insisted on the fact that the Jews were always considered as secondary in Morocco: in number and influence, but they had received good treatment form the Sultan and Muslim neighbors. Al-Maqri also explained to the Americans the role of the Sultan about the Jews during the application of Vichy law. The Americans were told that the German Armistice Committee that came to Morocco insisted on the necessity of treating the Jews in accordance with the requirements of the Nazi ideology.[351] This was strongly rejected by the Sultan, stressing that the relations between Jews and Muslims based on the long centuries of coexistence. Moreover, Muslims are in need of Jews and vice versa to preserve mutual formation of Moroccan culture and identity. Thus, in Morocco, there has never been a Jewish problem, and will not be in the future if the situation remains as it is now.[352]

[349] (May 11, 1891 – February 6, 1967), the U.S. Secretary of the Treasury during the administration of Franklin D. Roosevelt. https://en.wikipedia.org/wiki/Henry_Morgenthau,_Jr.(accessed 17/4/2016)

[350] Muhammad Kenbib, Sultan Sidi Mohammed Ben, http://www.minculture.gov.ma/index.php/2010-01-11-01-40-04/etudes-essaie/555-mohamed-kenbib-sultan-sidi-mohamed (accessed 18/4/2016).

[351] Robber Arsuf, *Moroccan Jews and Muhammad V*, 240-241.

[352] Muhammad Kenbib, Sultan Sidi Mohammed Ben Youssef, http://www.minculture.gov.ma/index.php/2010-01-11-01-40-04/etudes-essaie/555-mohamed-kenbib-sultan-sidi-mohamed. (accessed 3/22/2016).

The Moment of Preparation to Istiqlal and Jews.

Once the Jews overcame the dilemma of the Vichy law, they "faced the dilemma of being caught more and more between two the rival allegiances of two nationalist movements, Zionist and Moroccan, whose mobilization was accelerating towards independence" [353] in the following years between 1944 and 1955. These years, as Robber Assaraf indicates, witnessed the return of clashes and hostility between Muslims and Jews, especially in the aftermath of the establishment of the state of the Israel in 1948[354], "which further intensified the already ambivalent question of Moroccan Jewish identity."[355]

The arrival of American troops opened the door of Morocco wide for the American Jewish organizations to be more and more active in Morocco. They were interested in the issue of Jews of Morocco and their demographic weight in the prospect of building a Jewish state in Palestine. They began their activities by assimilating Jews into their claim, including the encouragement of emigration in a limited number from Morocco to Palestine.[356] Among these interests in the Moroccan Jews is the focus of the delegations who attended the World Jewish Congress in Atlantic City in November 1944 on the inhabitants of Moroccan *Mellah*.[357] Therefore, the delegations paid attention to the Jews who live in Morocco's *Mellah*s that

[353] Jonathan Wyrtzen, M.A, "Constructing Morocco", 264.
[354] Ibid.,265.
[355] Ibid.
[356] Muhammad Kenbib, Sultan Sidi Mohammed Ben Youssef, http://www.minculture.gov.ma/index.php/2010-01-11-01-40-04/etudes-essaie/555-mohamed-kenbib-sultan-sidi-mohamed (Accessed 24/3/2016).
[357] Jonathan Wyrtzen, M.A, "Constructing Morocco", 268.

can be relied upon to build the Jewish state.[358] It was for the first time that a Moroccan Jewish delegation attended such International Jewish conferences. Moroccan Jewish delegation presented "reports on the situation of Morocco's Jews in terms of education, housing, social problems, the reform of community organization, and political rights".[359] After the World War II, the W J C began his activity in favor of Moroccan Jews in which it made many pressures on the French authorities, "specifically to change the legal status of Moroccan Jews, renewing a campaign to grant Jews rights as French citizens."[360] In a letter of Leon Kubowitzki, the Secretary General of the W.J.C, to the French ambassador to the United States, Henri Bonnet, he complained about the situation when he compared it to the status of Moroccan Jews under French protectorate and Moroccan history. According to Wyrtzen, in this letter, Leon Kubowitzki showed that

> as "subjects" of the Sultan with less than full citizenship rights, the position of Moroccan Jews was actually worse under the French Protectorate than at other times in Moroccan history. Under the French, while positions were reserved for Muslims and French in the Sharifian government, Jews were prohibited from serving in the civil service. The letter went on to complain that Jewish courts had lost their autonomy since the arrival of the French, due to the fact that their jurisdiction had been limited to civil status cases, with all matters devolving to the Sharifian courts. He concluded by

---

[358] Muhammad Kenbib, Sultan Sidi Mohammed Ben Youssef, http://www.minculture.gov.ma/index.php/2010-01-11-01-40-04/etudes-essaie/555-mohamed-kenbib-sultan-sidi-mohamed (accessed 24/3/2016).

[359] Jonathan Wyrtzen, M.A, "Constructing Morocco", 268.

[360] Ibid.

calling for the Residency to put all Jewish civil and commercial cases under French law.[361]

On the eve of the World Jewish Congress in the Atlantic City, Moroccans people were celebrating the Throne Festival in 18 November 1944. The Sultan took this opportunity to remind Jews about his duties towards them as his subjects. This time, the Sultan violated the tradition on such occasions. He asked the Jewish delegation to get closer to him, and he stood for him and expressed his satisfaction towards Jews In his speech to Jews, he told them by saying: "you are my loyal subjects, you are like Muslims, and I like you and protect you, and the Muslims are still brothers and friends to you", and said, "this Eid is your Eid."[362] However, "the announcement of the United Nation's Palestine partition plan in December 1947"[363]increased the complexity of situation and hostility between the nationalists and Jews. To reduce these tensions, the Sultan met with the Jewish and Muslims figures and urged them "to continue to work together, stressing again that he did not have any distinction between his loyal subjects."[364] The ambivalence of Morocco's Jews about their identity was evident after the establishment of the state of Israel in 1948, despite the official proclamations that reassured them of their future, and their protection in Morocco. To avoid collisions and to reduce the impact of mutual recriminations between Muslims and Jews, the Sultan Muhammad V,

[361] Ibid.

[362] Muhammad Kenbib, Sultan Sidi Mohammed Ben Youssef, http://www.minculture.gov.ma/index.php/2010-01-11-01-40-04/etudes-essaie/555-mohamed-kenbib-sultan-sidi-mohamed. (accessed 25/3/2016).

[363] Jonathan Wyrtzen, M.A, "Constructing Morocco", 270.

[364] Muhammad Kenbib, Sultan Sidi Mohammed Ben Youssef , http://www.minculture.gov.ma/index.php/2010-01-11-01-40-04/etudes-essaie/555-mohamed-kenbib-sultan-sidi-mohamed. (accessed 25/3/2016).

delivered a radio address on May 23, 1948, strongly cautioning his subjects against any violence against the Moroccan Jewish population and urging them to distinguish between the events in Palestine and the situation of the Moroccan national community.[365]

After he explained his position about this issue and his support to his brothers "the Arab leaders", he declared:

> they [Muslim subjects] must know that the Moroccan Jews—who for centuries have resided in the country under the protection of its rulers, receiving the best welcome, and who have faithfully testified to their complete loyalty to the Moroccan throne—are different than the uprooted Jews who have been led from all the corners of the world towards Palestine, which they have unjustly and arbitrarily seized." In a note of warning that immediately followed, however, the Sultan warned his Jewish subjects to "avoid any sensitive act of supporting the Zionist aggression or manifesting any solidarity with it, because by doing so, they will threaten not only their individual rights but also their Moroccan nationality.[366]

However, despite these insurances from the Sultan Muhammad V, the year of 1949 witnessed the increase of the Jewish emigration to Palestine. The Zionist organizations were allowed to open a registration office in

[365] Jonathan Wyrtzen, M.A, "Constructing Morocco", 270
[366] Ibid.

Casablanca, "which began sending more than six hundred per month to Israel, a number that increased throughout the early 1950s."[367]

During the 1950s, the number of Jewish emigrants has risen significantly, especially after the exile of the Sultan to Madagascar. During this period, the protectorate used propaganda in trying to intimidate the Jews, claiming that the independence of Morocco would means persecution by Muslims. On the contrary, there were some Jews who engaged in nationalist parties and participate in the struggle for the return of the Sultan Muhammad V and to put an end to the era of protectorate.[368]

In Madagascar, during the period of negotiations in 1950 about his return to the throne, the Sultan discussed with the representatives of Moroccan parties (such as Hizb Istiqlal) the position of Moroccan Jews. The Sultan agreed, in case of formation of Moroccan Government, to consider the Jews equal to Muslims, and he would treat Jews and Muslims as equal citizens. The Sultan also discussed the issue of freedom of movement for Jews, where he agreed that it could be for all Jews citizens to leave the country.[369] The second half of 1955 witnessed many events relating to Jews. In August 1955, a Moroccan Jewish delegation went to France (Aix-les-Bains) to participate in negotiation about the future of Morocco after independence. Before starting negotiation, this delegation met with Moroccan nationalist delegation (Istiqlal party) to exchange their views about the future of Jews after independence. Concerning the future of Jews,

---

[367] Ibid.,275.

[368] Muhammad Kenbib, Sultan Sidi Mohammed Ben Youssef, http://www.minculture.gov.ma/index.php/2010-01-11-01-40-04/etudes-essaie/555-mohamed-kenbib-sultan-sidi-mohamed .(accessed 25/3/2016).

[369] Robber Arsuf, *Moroccan Jews and Muhammad V*, 305.

the nationalists promised to establish a constitutional monarchy based on a group of basic principles. Among these principles is the equality in rights and duties between all Moroccans without any racial or religious distinction.[370] In 16 October 1955, at Rabat, the Regency (*Majlis al-Wisaya 'ala al-'Arsh*) was founded. At this occasion, it was declared that Morocco would move into a new democratic era providing for all Moroccans, whatever their religion, equality in rights and duties.[371]

After the return of the Sultan from Madagascar to Paris in 30 October, 1955, he received many congratulations from the Moroccan Jews either from Morocco or France. For example, in 2 November 1955, the Sultan met with the Jew Ohana as representative of Jewish nationalists in Morocco. In 5 November, the Sultan met with some of members of the Counsel of Jewish communities and the inspector of Moroccan Jewish institutions. In 7 November, the Sultan met with a delegation of Moroccan Rabbis among them the president of the Supreme Court of the Rabbis. In all of these meetings, the Sultan reassured Jews that they would live in a full equality and freedom as well as confirmed that the Jews become Moroccan citizens and would enjoy full citizenship by force of the law like Muslim citizens, so the Jews would have the same rights as Muslims without any discrimination.[372]

In 1956, when Morocco got independence, the attitude of Muhammad V towards Jews was honorable in which he granted the Jews political rights.

[370] Muhammad Hatimi, "the Moroccan Jewish Communities and the last ways leading to the independence of Morocco", 73.

[371] Ibid.,306.

[372] Ibib,.311-312.

In the first words of the Sultan when he arrived to Morocco reassured the Jews would become citizens, affirming that Jews would be granted full citizenship under the law.[373] As a result, the Government's constitution assured equality between Jews and Muslims and put an end implicitly and officially to the status of dhimmi. The appointment of the famous Jewish Doctor, Leon Benzaquen, as a Minister of the Posts and Telegraphs in the first Moroccan Government "was a symbol of the Jewish community's importance". In addition, three Jews were elected to Parliament as well as many Jews were appointed in high posts in the administration and industry. After the declaration of independence, Muslims and Jews gathered in a movement known as al-Wifaq. In a declaration in 1956, "al-Wifaq proclaimed: here in Morocco there are only Moroccan citizens: Moroccans of the Muslim religion and Moroccans of the Jewish religion, but all are Moroccans".[374]

Conclusion

The purpose of this chapter was to explore the legal status of Moroccan Jews during the French protectorate period. It focuses only on Jews who were under French authorities. This chapter examines the policy of French authorities towards Jews and explores how French dealt with the issue of Moroccan Jews to keep them in their traditional status. It argues that the legal status of Jews under the French authorities was very complicated and ambiguous. The legal reforms in the Jews' status were designed by French authorities was more to control Jews rather than to

[373] Ibid,.313.

[374] Daniel J. Schroeter, "The Shifting Boundaries of Moroccan Jewish Identities", issue 15, no. 1 (fall 2008):159.

improve their situation. The aim of French authorities, as chapter indicates, was to gain the support of the *Makhzan*, especially *'ulama* on one hand, and also to mobilize Jews on the other to success in its mission. In addition, this chapter argued that the legal status of Jews became more complicated in 1941 under Vichy law. It illustrates how Jews, at that time, used the status of *Dhimmi* to escape Vichy law, in which they asked the Sultan Muhammad V to protect them in accordance with the Dhimma system. Relating to the attitude of the *Makhzan*, this chapter highlights the changing attitude of the *Makhzan* and Muslim nationalists about Jews. It argues that the *Makhzan* began to use a new language of "equality" and citizens in its formal speech to mobilize more Jews. Following the exile of the Sultan to Madagascar, the chapter mentions the role of the nationalists to convince Jews about the future of Jews in Morocco, affirming that Morocco would become for all Moroccans both Jews and Muslims. In this respect, Jews participated in negotiations that held in Aix-les-Bains in France in August 1955 about independence of Morocco and the return of the Sultan Muhammad V to the throne. Through these negotiations Jews received assurances about their status in the state. In 1956 the year of the independence of Morocco, the first Moroccan Government's constitution assured equality between Jews and Muslims and put an end implicitly and officially to the status of *dhimmi*.

Conclusion

The goal of this book has been to demonstrate how and why Moroccan Jews were defined at independence in 1956 as Moroccan citizens, putting an end to the old legal system in which they lived under through the centuries. This book attempted to chart the approach between change and continuity in analyzing the Moroccan Jewish struggle to get status as citizens. By first examining "how" the legal status of Jews was before 1856, this book looks back at the history of the emergence of the *dhimma* system. As discussed in the first chapter, the preliminary principles that determined the legal status of non-Muslims emerged after the death of the Prophet Muhammad (PBUH). It was argued that the *dhimma* system was the result of many circumstances that happened in the first centuries that followed the era of the Prophet. By the establishment of the first Muslim state in Madina, the relationship between Muslims and non-Muslims (Jews) living in *al-Madīna* was determined by the so-called *ṣaḥīfat al-Madīna*. Because the Jews were composed a large proportion of the population in Medina, *ṣaḥīfat al-Madīna* considered them indigenous citizens in which they was forming one nation with Muslims. However, following the death of Prophet, many political and economic factors led finally to a second constitutional text (the pact of 'Umar) that Islamic jurisprudence based on in codifying the legal status of Jews later. This book brought out three versions of this document. The aim was to show the differences of the contents of these versions in Islamic legal heritage arguing that this text is only a result of the diligence (*ijtihad*) of jurists who attributed it to 'Umar b. Khattāb to gather a legal force. In this regard, this book discussed the modern scholars' view about the legal status of non-Muslims living in Muslim societies. Modern scholars proclaimed that there is now the need of creating a new understanding to the dhimma system by referring to the Document of Medina as a model of dealing with the diversity does exist in Muslim communities.

In terms of the changing legal status of Jews in Morocco, the contribution of this book has been to examine "how and why" Moroccan Jews were defined at independence as Moroccan citizens. To answer these two questions, this book examines, in second chapter, the factors that contributed to the changes that took place in the legal status of Jews in Moroccan Islam. It was argued that the growing penetration of the European powers in Morocco had an essential contribution to the transformation of Jews from the nationals of the Sultan to a problem (protégés/foreign protection). The second chapter focuses on two things that had big impacts on the legal status of Jews during the second half of the nineteenth century. The first is the emergence of the issue of foreign protection, which was an essential issue that indicated the inability of the Sultan to control his nationals. Second is in the international political support which Jews took advantage of in their relations with Europeans. Through this examination, it was clearly that these two things contributed to the legal and political emancipation of Jews from Islamic law, represented by the sultan. On the other hand, this book argues the legal status of Jews in this period had seen considerable deterioration because, instead, they obtained new reforms in their status; they became subjects or protégés of European countries.

Finally, in chapter three, this book discussed the legal status of Moroccan Jews under French authorities. In this respect, this thesis argues that the legal status of Jews under the French authorities was very complicated and ambiguous. The legal reforms in the Jews' status were designed by French authorities was more to control Jews rather than to improve their situation. It was mentioned that the aim of French authorities was to gain the support of the *Makhzan*, especially '*ulama* on one hand, and also to mobilize Jews on the other to success in its mission. Therefore, Jews did not obtain new status during the French protectorate. However, in 1941 under the Vichy law, the status of Jews became more complicated. To avoid the Vichy law, Jews asked the Sultan Muhammad V to protect them in accordance with the Dhimma law. Concerning the *Makhzan*, this thesis argues that it began to use a new discourse of "equality" and citizens in its formal speech to mobilize more Jews. In terms of their struggle against the French protectorate, this thesis mentions the role of the nationalists to convince Jews about the future of Jews in Morocco, affirming that Morocco would become for all Moroccans both Jews and Muslims. In this respect, Jews participated in negotiations held in Aix-les-Bains in France in August 1955 about independence of Morocco and the return of the Sultan Muhammad V to the throne. Through these negotiations, Jews received assurances about their status in new monarchy that will establish after independence. This is what happened in 1956 the year of the independence of Morocco, in which the first Moroccan Government's constitution assured equality between Jews and Muslims and put an end implicitly and officially to the status of *dhimmi*.

BIBLIOGRAPHY

Abu-Manneh, Butrus. 1994. "The Islamic Roots of the Gülhane Rescript." *Die Welt Des Islams* 34, no. 2 (November, 1994): 173–203.

Al-Bachir, Tariq. "About the Conditions of Participation in the Public Affairs of State to non-Muslims in Contemporary Islamic Societies." *Journal of Modern Muslim* 69 and 72, no. 5 (January 2, 1994).

Al-Najdi, Abd al-Rahmān. *Ahkām 'aqd al-Amān wa-al Musta'min fi al-Islam*. Riyad: 1990.

Al-Nasiri, Ahmed, *Kitāb al-Isti9sa fi al-Maghreb al-9sa*. Casablanca: Dar al-Kitāb, 1956.

Al-Ghazali, Muhammad. *Intolerance and tolerance between Christianity and Islam*. Cairo: 2000.

Al-Harithi, Turki Ajlan. "The Changing status of Jews in Morocco in the Nineteenth Century and the attitude of the Moroccan government." *Historical Studies Journal* 45, 46 (1993): 187-213.

Al-Sghir Khalid. *Morocco and Great Britain in the Nineteenth Century 1856-1886*. Casablanca: al-Najah al-Jadida, 1997.

Al-Qaradawi, Yusuf. "The Rights of non-Muslim Minority." The *Journal of al-Tawhid* 84 (1955).

______. *Non-Muslims in Muslim Society*. Cairo: Library of Wahba, 1977.

Alon, Ilia. "Dhimma", *Encyclopedia of the Modern Middle East and North Africa* (2004), *Encyclopedia.com*, http://www.encyclopedia.com/doc/1G2-3424600816.html (accessed April 18, 2016).

Al-Zayn, Hassān. *al-Awdā' al-Qānuniyya Li al-Nasārā wa' al-Yahud fi al-Diyar al-Islamiyya hattā al-Fath al-'Uthmani* [the Legal Conditions of the Chrisians and Jews in Islamic Lands up to the Ottman Conquests]. Beiru,.t, 1988.

Al-Zhili,Wahba. "The Concept of Citizenship in the Islamic Perspective." *Islamiyat* (2 October 2012). http://www.islameiat.com/Pages/Subjects/Default.aspx?id=15181&cat_id=107 (accessed April 18, 2016).

Assaraf, Robert. *Mohammed V et les juifs du Maroc à l'époque de Vichy*. Paris: Plon, 1997.

Ayache, Germain. "Jewish Minority in Pre-Colonial Morocco", *Revue Dar al-Niaba : études d'histoire marocaine* 12 (1986): 6-26.

B. 'Abud, Muhammad. *The History of Morocco*. Tetouan: 1951.

Bin-Nun, Yigal. "The Contribution of World Jewish Organizations to the Establishment of Rights for Jews in Morocco (1956-1961)." *Journal of Modern Jewish Studies* 9, no. 2 (July 2010): 251-274.

Bossenga, Gail. "Citizenship: Europe, 1450 to 1789." *Encyclopedia of the Early Modern World* (2004), *Encyclopedia.com*. http://www.encyclopedia.com/doc/1G23404900219.html (accessed April 18, 2016).

Boum, Aomar. *Memories of Absence: How Muslims Remember Jews in Morocco*. Stanford: Stanford University Press, 2013.

_____. "From 'Little Jerusalems' to the Promised Land: Zionism, Moroccan Nationalism and Rural Jewish Emigration." *Journal of North African Studies* 15, no. 1 (March 2010):51- 69

_____."Colonial Minorities: Jewish-Muslim relations in southern Morocco re-evaluated." *Hesperis-Tamuda* Vol XLVIII, (2013): 25-40.

b. Mansur, Abd al-Wahab. *The Problem of the Consulate Protection: From its Establishment into the Madrid Conference in 1888*. Rabat: 1985.

Chouraqui, Andre. *The Social and Legal Status of the Jews of French Morocco*. New York: American Jewish Committee, 1953.

_____.*La Condition Juridique de L'Israelite Marocain*. Paris: 1950.

Cohen, Amine. "Tujjar al-Sultan: Nukhab Yhudiyya fi Maghrib of the Nineteenth Century Nukhab Maghāribīyah: al-Marji'īyāt, al-Masārāt wa al-Adwār", edited by *Ibn Abdallāwī, al-Mukhtār* (2012):79-94.

Cohen, Mark R. "What was the Pact of 'Umar? Literally Historical Studies". *JSAI* 23 (1999).

_____.*Under Crescent and Cross: the Jews in the Middle Ages*. New Jersey: 1994.

Corcos, David. "The Jews of Morocco under the Marinides." *The Jewish Quarterly Review*, New Series 54, no. 4 (Apr., 1964): 271-287.

Encyclopædia Britannica Online, s. v. "Muhammad V." http://www.britannica.com/biography/Muhammad-V-sultan-of-Morocco (accessed April 18, 2016).

El Mansour, Mohamed. *Morocco in the reign of Mawaly Sulayman*. Middle East & North African Studies Press, 1990.

El-Messiri, Abd al-Wahab. *Jews, Judaism and Zionism encyclopedia*. Volume 4. Cairo: 1999.

Fattal, Antoine. Le statut légal des non-musulmans en pays d'Islam. Dar al-Machreq Sarl : 1995.

_____.*Le statut légal des Musulmans en Pays d'Islam*. Bierut: Impromerie catholique, 1958.

Ghannouchi, Rached. *Public freedoms in the Islamic state*. Beirut: Central studies for Arab Unity, 1998.

Gold, Rick. "Arab and Berber Dynasties from the 7th to the 17th Century." http://rickgold.home.mindspring.com/page8.html (accessed 12/12/2015).

Gilson Miller, Susan. *A History of Modern Morocco*. Cambridge University Press, 2013.

Girgis, Magdy. *Coptic Judiciary in Egypt*. Cairo: 1999.

Hatimi, Muhammad. "Moroccan Jewish Groups in Scholarly Research". *Religion et Société en Afrique* : le débat. Rabat : Institut des études africaines, 2009, 9-24.

______."The Moroccan Jewish Communities and the Last Ways Leading to Independence of Morocco", in *the Negotiation of Aix Liban and Moroccan Independence,* 73-87. Rabat, 2008.

Howeidi, Fahmi. *Citizens not Dhimmis*. Cairo: Dar al-Shuru9, 1999.

Hunwick, John. *Jews of a Saharan Oasis: Eliminations of the Tamantit Community*. Princeton: Markus Wiener Publishers, 2006

Ibn Hibban, Muhammad. *الثقات (Trustworthy)*. The Ministry of Knowledge high for the government of India: 1978.

Ibn Qayyim al-Jawziyyah, Muhammad ibn Abu Bakr. *Ahkam ahl al-Dhimma*. Beirut: Dar Ibn Hazm, 2008.

Ibn Khaldūn, Abd al-Rahman (d. 1406), *Kitāb* al-*'ibar* [*Tarikh ibn Khaldūn*]. Beirut: Dar al-Fikr, 2000.

Ibn Manzur, Muhammad. *Lisan al-'Arab* [the Arab tongue]. Beirut, 1990, Volume, 15.

Ibn 'Idhārī, Muhammad. Kitāb al-Bayān al-Mughrib fī akhbār al-Andalus wa-al-Maghrib [Taḥqiq wa-murāja'at G S Colin; Evariste Lévi-Provençal; Iḥsān 'Abbās], Volume 4. Beirut: Dār al-Thaqāfah, 1983.

Ibrahim Hassan, Hassan. *Tarikh al-Islam*, V. 1. Beirut: Dar al-Jil, 1991.

Isaac Azayan, Ramadan. "'Umar's pact Narratives: Documental Study." The *Journal of the Islamic University* (Islamic Studies Series) Volume XIV, issue 2 (June: 2006): 169-203.

Joseph Tobi; Y Barnay; Shalom Bar-Asher; Samuel Ettinger; Michel Abitbol. *Al-Yahūd fī al-Buldān al-Islāmīyah, 1850-1950*. Al-Kuwayt: al-Majlis al-Waṭanī lil-Thaqāfah wa-al-Funūn wa- al-Ādāb, 1995.

Kahila, Abd al-Rahman. *The Covenant of Umar: A New Reading*. Cairo: 1996.

Kenbib, Mohammed. *Juifs et Musulmans au Maroc, 1859-1948: contribution à l'histoire des relations inter-communautaires en terre d'Islam*. Casablanca: Imprimerie Najah El Jadida, 1994.

_____."The Sultan Sidi Mohammed Ben Youssef between History and Collective Memory of Jews." http://www.minculture.gov.ma/index.php/2010-01-11-01-40-04/etudes-essaie/555-mohamed-kenbib-sultan-sidi-mohamed (accessed 16/3/2016).

Khalaf, Abd al-Wahhab. *Islamic Politics* [*al-Siyāsā al-Shar'iya*]. Cairo: 1932.

Lévy, Simon. *Essais d'histoire et de civilisation judeo-marocains*. Rabat: Centre Tarik Ibn Zyad, 2001.

_____."The Jewish Community in the Framework of the History of Morocco: from the 17th Century to the last 20th Century. In *Identity and dialogue, Modern and Contemporary History of the Jews of Morocco* 25-85. Rabat: Dar Al Stoki: 1982.

Lévy, Armand. *Il Etait une Fois les Juifs Marocains : Témoignage et histoire de la vie quotidienne*. Paris : Harmattan, 1995.

Mahdi Shams al-Din, Muhammad. *The Islamic-Christian Dialogue/about a Project for Joint Struggle*. Beirut: 2004. http://www.almaaref.org/books/contentsimages/books/dirasat/al_muwatana/page/lesson4.htm.

March Andrew F. *Islam and Liberal Citizenship: the Search for an Overlapping Consensus*. Oxford University Press, 2009.

Martin, Evans. "Algeria's Jewish Question". *History Today* 62, no.7 (Juley 2012):10-16.

Marglin, Jessica. 'Aspects de la modernité judiciaire au Maroc : protégés juifs, tribunaux consulaires et loi islamique.' In *La bienvenue et l'adieu Migrants juifs et musulmans au Maghreb* (XVe-XXe siècle), Vo. 1 (2010) :167-189.

Meyers, Alan R. "Patronage and protection: the status of Jews in precolonial Morocco", in S. Deshen and W.P. Zenner (eds). *Jewish Societies in the Middle East*. Washington DC: University Press of America (1982): 83-97.

Mubaarakfoori, Wasfi al-Rahman. *Sealed Nectar in the Prophet's Biography*. Qatar: 2007.

Reda, Muhammad. *Muhammad Rasul Allah*. Beirut: 2006.

Salim al-'Awa, Muhammad. *Religion and the Homeland: Chapters in the Relation Between Muslims and non-Muslims*. Cairo: Dar Nahdet, 2009.

_____."Dhimmis in the Islamic legal system, contemporary Islamic vision." *The Journal of the good life* 32, no. 11, 2003.

Schroeter, Daniel J. "From Dhimmis to Colonized Subjects: Moroccan Jews and the Sharifian and French Colonial State". *Studies in Contemporary Jewry*, 19 (2003), 104-123.

_____and Joseph Chetrit, "Emancipation and its Discontents: Jews at the formative Period of Colonial Rule in Morocco." *Jewish Social Studies*: History, Culture, Society n. s. 13, no. 1 (Fall 2006): 170–206.

_____."The Shifting Boundaries of Moroccan Jewish Identities". *Jewish Social Studies: History, Culture, Society* n.s. 15, no. 1 (Fall 2008):145–64.

_____. "On the Origins and Identity of Indigenous North African Jews: A Cultural Reappraisal of Ethnic and Religious Minorities". in N Boudraa & J Krause (eds), *North African Mosaic: A Cultural Reappraisal of Ethnic and Religious Min,* 164-17. Cambridge Scholars Press, Newcastle, 2.

_____.*The Sultan's Jew: Morocco and Sephardi World*. Stanford University Press: 2002.

_____."Royal Power and the Economy in Precolonial Morocco: Jews and the Legitimation of Foreign Trade," *In the Shadow of the Sultan: Culture, Power and Politics in Morocco.*", edited by Rahma Bourqia and Susan Gilson Miller, 74-102. *Harvard University Press*, 1999.

Sha'ibi, Ahmed. *Document of Medina: the Content and Significance*. Qatar: Published by the Nation book, volume 110, 2006.

Shaw, Stanford J. "The History of the Ottoman Empire and Modern Turkey." *The Oxford Encyclopedia of the Islamic World.* http://www.oxfordislamicstudies.com/article/opr/t236/e0611# (accessed 12/8/2015).

Shiḥātah Rayyah, 'Aṭā 'Alī Muḥammad. *al-Yahūd fī bilād al-Maghrib al-Aqṣa' fī 'Ahd al-Marīnīyīn Wa-al-Waṭṭāsīyīn*. Dimashq : Dār al-Kalimah, 1999.

Stillman, Norman A. *The Jews of Arab Lands in Modern Times*. New York: the Jewish

Publication Society, 1991.

Tahir-ul-Qadri, Muhammad. "The Constitution of Medina: 63 Constitutional Articles." London: Minhaj-ul-Quran Publications, 2012: 1-16. http://www.minhajpublications.com/wp-content/uploads/2014/01/The_Constitution_of_Madina_Ebook.pdf.

Tahtah, Muhammad. "Brothers Enemies: the Jews of Morocco in the Modern era."(16 /01/2012). http://www.hespress.com/orbites/45471.html (accessed 10/28/2015).

Thompson, Elizabeth. "*jizya*." Encyclopedia of the Modern Middle East and North Africa. (2004). Encyclopedia.com. http://www.encyclopedia.com/doc/1G2-3424601439.html (accessed 18 April. 2016).

Tsur, Yaron. "Moroccan Jewry and Decolonization: A Modern History of Collective Social Boundaries", Borders and Boundaries in and around Dutch Jewish History, Edited by Judith Frishman, David J. Wertheim, Ido de Haan and Joel Cahen, *Amsterdam University Press.* Amsterdam, 2011: 193-200.

Tobi, Joseph; Y Barnay; Shalom Bar-Asher; Samuel Ettinger; Michel Abitbol, *al-Yahūd fī al-Buldān al-Islāmīyah [the Jews in Muslim Countries], 1850-1950*. al-Kuwayt: al-Majlis al-Waṭanī lil-Thaqāfah wa-al-Funūn wa- al-Ādāb, 1995.

Vance, Sharon, *The Martyrdom of a Moroccan Jewish Saint*, Brill's Series in Jewish Studies, V. 44, 2011.

Warren, David H. and Gilmore, Christine. "Rethinking neo-Salafism through an Emerging Fiqh of Citizenship: The Changing Status of Minorities in the Discourse of Yusuf al-Qaradawi and the 'School of the Middle Way." *New Middle Eastern Studies*, issue 2,(29 October 2012), 1-7, http://www.brismes.ac.uk/nmes/wp-content/uploads/2012/10/NMES2012WarrenGilmore.pdf.

Welfensohn, Israel. *The history of Jews in Arab Countries*. Egypt: 1927.

Wyrtzen, Jonathan David. "Constructing Morocco: The Colonial Struggle to define the Nation, 1912-1956." PhD diss., Georgetown University, 2009.

Ya'coubi, *The history of Ya'coubi*. Beirut: 2010.

Zafrani, Haim. *Two Thousands Years of Jewish Life in Morocco*. Jersey City, NJ: KTAV, 2005.

Zaydan, Abd al- Karim. *Al-Dmmiin wa-al Musta'min fi Dar al-Islam*. Beirut: Maktbat al-9uds, 1982.

Table of Contents

MIX
Papier aus verantwortungsvollen Quellen
Paper from responsible sources
FSC® C105338

Printed by Books on Demand GmbH, Norderstedt / Germany